Major Edward E. Hartwick

# *A Biographical Sketch*

## *of*

# Major Edward E. Hartwick

TOGETHER WITH A
COMPILATION OF MAJOR HARTWICK'S LETTERS
AND DIARIES WRITTEN DURING THE
SPANISH-AMERICAN AND
WORLD WARS

*Gordon K. Miller*

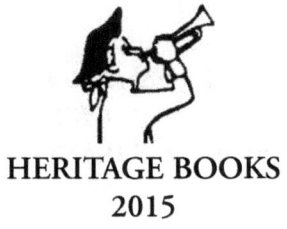

HERITAGE BOOKS
2015

# HERITAGE BOOKS
*AN IMPRINT OF HERITAGE BOOKS, INC.*

### Books, CDs, and more—Worldwide

For our listing of thousands of titles see our website
at
www.HeritageBooks.com

A Facsimile Reprint
Published 2015 by
HERITAGE BOOKS, INC.
Publishing Division
5810 Ruatan Street
Berwyn Heights, Md. 20740

Originally published 1921
Detroit, Michigan

— Publisher's Notice —
In reprints such as this, it is often not possible to remove blemishes from the original. We feel the contents of this book warrant its reissue despite these blemishes and hope you will agree and read it with pleasure.

International Standard Book Numbers
Paperbound: 978-0-7884-5127-0
Clothbound: 978-0-7884-9280-8

# MAJOR EDWARD E. HARTWICK

## Chapter I

TO MEMORIALIZE and record, by the written word, the simple story of one who exemplified the very best qualities of American manhood is the purpose of this volume. Our national historical literature is replete with the records of men who, like Major Hartwick, possessed to the fullest degree those qualities which indicate exceptional character and ability. Major Hartwick's life was one of vivid experience through two wars, of service to his fellows, devoted attention to his family and honorable participation in business affairs. To have known Major Hartwick was to love and respect his sterling worth, his Christian conception of life, his fairness, generosity and democratic disposition. One has but to read the estimates of him from persons in every walk of life to appreciate the universal regard held for him. Trained in military discipline, yet he tempered his command with fatherly kindness and consideration for the man in the ranks; in business he exercised the same precision and thoroughness of action as he had in the service of his country, and in both fields he was eminently successful. Modest and utterly devoid of ego, Major Hartwick refrained from attaching publicity to the interesting events of his career. His letters and diaries written during his service in both the Spanish-American and World Wars are invaluable, not only historically, but in showing the thoughts of one engaged in the grim business of war. Major Hartwick was a scholar, a lover of the aesthetic, an interested and keen observer of life and people. Endowed with a natural brilliancy of intellect, he acquired his education easily, even through the rigid curriculum of the United States Military Academy. After his graduation, however, his life was one of action and close attention to his military and business

duties without opportunity to engage in those pleasures, or avocations, which were really very close to his heart, and it was his desire, had he survived, to do those things which circumstances had compelled him to neglect. Yet a man young in years and thought, he had served his country well; in business pursuits he had "made good"; he was blessed with an ideal home and family; he counted his friends by the number of those who knew him, and life in prospect held much, but Providence, in one of His moods which we do not understand, ordained that to his flag he should give that "last full measure of devotion"—his life.

Edward Edgar Hartwick was born September 6, 1871, at the town of St. Louis, Michigan, one of the three children of Michael Shoat and Jane Augusta (Obear) Hartwick.

The family of Hartwick is one of the oldest in America. One of the first of the name to come to this country was John Christopher Hartwick, a native of Saxe-Gotha, Germany, born January 6, 1714, educated for the Lutheran ministry in the University of Halle, and while a young man sailed to America as a missionary to the Indians. The exact date of his coming is not known, but in 1746, he was the pastor of St. Peter's Lutheran Church at Rhinebeck, New York, serving nearly all of the western and northern part of what is now the Empire State. After over fifty years of service, he died in 1796, leaving, as he supposed, about 20,000 acres in what is now Hartwick Township, Otsego County, New York, for the foundation of a "Gymnasium, Seminale Theologium and Missionarium" and also a "College Gymnasium and Seminary." This large tract of land had been purchased directly from the Indians under a patent of the governor, the deed of which is preserved in the Cooperstown museum. Reverend Hartwick had in view the establishment of a school where preparation might be secured for missionary work among the savages. However, through some unforeseen cause, the value of the estate dwindled and only the sum of $16,000 was available for the trustees of the proposed school. Notwithstanding this fact, on

September 15, 1797, Hartwick Seminary was founded and today exists in all prosperity as the oldest Lutheran school in America and one of the oldest of all denominational schools in this country. It is located in the beautiful valley of the Susquehanna River, in Otsego County, four miles from Cooperstown.

The progenitor in this country of the direct line of Edward E. Hartwick was John Burt Hartwick, a brother of John Christopher Hartwick, the Lutheran missionary. John B. Hartwick was born in Germany about the year 1756, and came to America in 1764. He settled in New York State and during the War of the Revolution he fought in the American Army until surrender of Cornwallis at Yorktown. The next in the line was Peter Hartwick, born in New York State in 1784, followed by Nelson Hartwick, who was born on the Ottawa River in Canada in 1812, and became the father of a large family of children, among whom was Michael S. Hartwick, the father of Edward E. Michael S. Hartwick was born in 1841, located at Grayling, Michigan, in an early day and died in the year 1909.

The boyhood life of Edward E. Hartwick was much the same as that of any other American youth. As a lad he indulged in the sports of his chums with enthusiasm and was equally as fond of his books; he was ever respectful of his elders and took to heart well the teachings of his father and mother. That he was fortunate in having the splendid rearing that he had, there is no doubt, but those who guided him through the tender years were well repaid to witness the result of their labors—a perfect specimen of up-standing young manhood, a credit to himself and his community. Edward Hartwick received his early education in the graded schools and, in 1888, graduated from the Grayling High School, ranking at the head of his class both in yearly class work and in June examinations. That the young student had been interested in things of military nature is indicated by the subject of an address prepared at this time: "The Cost of Military Glory" was the title and his treatment of the subject might be epitomized by Gray's immortal line, "The paths of glory lead but to the grave." Another manuscript written by him at this time, when he was fifteen years of age, upon "Socialism and Anarchism," is one that might easily have been composed by a maturer mind. But young Hartwick was a thinker beyond his years; he had that happy faculty of absorbing knowledge and the keen desire to find and learn new things, a trait which never left him. Somehow the thought of this young man, studying in the late hours of the night, calls up another picture, that of an officer in 1917, pacing the hurricane deck of a transport en route overseas—and studying French as he walked. This unwillingness to lose a moment, unnecessarily, characterized Edward E. Hartwick throughout his life.

At this point in young Hartwick's life there arose the necessity of choosing a career. Army service had always appealed strongly to him, as some member of his family had fought in every American war. Consequently, when there came the opportunity to receive an appointment to the United States Military Academy, he eagerly embraced it. He entered school at West Point September 1, 1889. During his four years in the academy his experiences were those common to the average student in that institution.

As every West Pointer well knows, the life of the newcomer at the Academy is no flower-strewn path. Quite the reverse. But young Hartwick endured the hardships imposed upon him with rare sportsmanship, and by so doing won many friends. Just a few days after he entered the Academy, September 15, 1889, he wrote:

"I am now a 'new cadet' or, as we are dubbed here, a 'Sep.' There are 16 of us left out of the 57 that were here when I wrote before. The result of the exam was made known Saturday and on Monday our recitations in mathematics and English began. We have two hours and a half for recitations, two hours for drill, one hour and a half for meals, an hour studying the rules and regulations, and the rest of the time for study. Reveille is at 5:30 a. m., when we must be up, and taps at 10 p. m., when we must be in bed. No time for play here. Last week our 'plebe skins' were issued to us. We look like a crowd of overgrown children in them. When we go across the area with our hands flattened out, the palms to the front, we look ridiculous enough. We will have to walk that way till October 1st. Then we can don the dress-coat with 46 brass buttons on it, and will then have arisen from the condition of a beast to that of a 'plebe.' We won't be treated like 'things' *then*. Last week we took the 'oath' and Friday our 'warrants' were given us. Our rifles were given us then and we don't get the tedious squad drill any more. You have no idea of the amount of work the name 'Sep' implies, or the amount of 'jumping' it expresses. I wish I could tell you of the fun *'they'* have with us. It would fill a book if written. They had me dancing in a smile for 15 minutes this morning. They *accidentally* hanged a 'Sep' last week. We don't get much time for study."

Upon another occasion the paternal head of the family journeyed to West Point to see his son. But Cadet Hartwick was "walking the area"—and could not be seen, even by his own father. That Hartwick received demerits is certain; they are inevitable, but the records show that he upheld the best traditions of the school and was graduated June 12, 1893, with high honors. His official number upon the West Point roll is 3547.

Having chosen the cavalry branch of the service, Edward E. Hartwick was appointed second lieutenant in the 3rd Cavalry on June 12, 1893, was transferred to the 4th Cavalry July 26th, following, and on August 5th was assigned to the 9th United States Cavalry (colored). With the famous fighting 9th he remained throughout his service. The 9th had been organized in the year 1866 at New Orleans and the recruits were the pick of the black race. The fighting qualities of these big, ebony-hued men were proved soon afterwards in the campaigns against Indians and outlaws in the West. To this command, stationed at Fort Robinson, Nebraska, Lieutenant Hartwick was sent in September, 1893. Throughout his six years with the old 9th, Lieutenant Hartwick was always proud of his men and he was equally well liked by them. Such a command was not the easiest, in fact it was one of the hardest, and it is a tribute to the personality and leadership of the lieutenant that he was successful. In 1895 he served with his command in the Bannock campaign in Idaho and Wyoming, in the Jackson Hole country, as second lieutenant of "E" Troop and as squadron adjutant under Major Adna R. Chaffee, who, by the way, was one of the closest friends whom Lieutenant Hartwick made during his service with the 9th. From September, 1897, until April, 1898, Lieutenant Hartwick was a student officer at the Infantry and Cavalry School at Fort Leavenworth, Kansas, and in this connection it is interesting to quote from a letter written to him by Chaffee, which shows the esteem the veteran held for the young officer:

"I have your letter of recent date, also the map, for both of which I am greatly obliged. The map speaks for itself and is but the visible evidence of the care and thorough performance of a duty that I felt certain would be the result when the work was intrusted to you for execution. You are not of those who slight duty because disagreeable and at times require hard work, and I believe you take much satisfaction in doing your work well and willingly. In the long run you will be compensated, as you will find from your own personal observation. I will venture the remark now that both Department and War Department will appreciate the intelligence and labor you bestowed in gathering the information necessary for so much detail as exhibited in the map."

From Fort Leavenworth, Lieutenant Hartwick was ordered to join his command at Chickamauga, Georgia, which he did on April 23rd. This was the beginning of his Spanish-American service, in which his brilliant conduct and courage won the approbation of his superior officers. He remained throughout the campaign with Troop "H," and as acting regimental adjutant; also, from July 26th to August 13th, 1898, as acting chief quartermaster of the Cavalry Division, 5th Army Corps, under General Wheeler. For distinguished service at San Juan he was promoted in May of the following year to the rank of first lieutenant.

Of the campaign before Santiago and the events in connection, and of Lieutenant Hartwick's participation therein, we refer to the published diaries, letters, official reports and the reports of his superior officers appended to this sketch. No contemporaneous literature of the Spanish-American War holds more of interesting detail, genuine heart interest and colorful description than Lieutenant Hartwick's personal accounts. Aside from their interest, they form a valuable contribution to history, as there are certain accepted facts, which have come to be of general belief, which are proved to be in error by these reports.

A glimpse of the meritorious service performed by Lieutenant Hartwick during the torrid day of July 1, 1898, before San Juan Hill, may be had by reading from the official report of Lieutenant M. M. McNamee, of the 9th Cavalry, commanding Troop "H":

> "The country is covered with dense undergrowth and great caution had to be exercised to avoid being ambushed by the enemy. In this connection much credit is due 2nd Lieutenant Hartwick, 9th Cavalry, who conducted the movements of the 'point' and 'flankers' in the advance. Lieutenant Hartwick pushed steadily forward until he was fired on by the enemy and directed by me to halt. This officer displayed great coolness in a very trying and dangerous position. During the assault and throughout the entire day, by his courage and prompt action, I was enabled to get the best result from the troop. I recommend him for consideration."

During the day of the fight at San Juan, Lieutenant Hartwick first came into contact with Colonel Theodore Roosevelt, commanding part of the 1st Volunteer Cavalry or the "Rough Riders." It is not our purpose to question in the least the veracity of such a man as Theodore Roosevelt, and if any statements of the latter conflict with the real facts, possibly they might be attributed to his natural enthusiasm and regard for his own men and his intense desire to award them all the credit possible. From the accounts written by Lieutenant Hartwick, and Captain E. D. Dimmick of the 9th, also that of Lieutenant McNamee, it will be seen that when Colonel Roosevelt, mounted, arrived at the line held by the 9th and 1st regulars at the foot of San Juan Hill, he was in a quandary as to just what to do. He had with him a skirmish line of the Rough Riders.

In later years, when describing this incident to his family and friends, Major Hartwick stated that Colonel Roosevelt and he were talking together when the call was sounded and in the din and confusion it was not heard clearly by either of them, whereupon Colonel Roosevelt inquired, "What was that call?" This question Lieutenant Hartwick repeated to Private Prince (who was killed on that day) and the latter, who was standing at some distance away, shouted, "It's the charge, sir," at the same time starting forward. Lieutenant Hartwick then repeated the order to Roosevelt. The troops then attacked and carried the hill. They advanced, or charged, as a mixed unit, each man, whether regular or volunteer, black or white, intent only on reaching the top.

In his own account of the incident in "The Rough Riders," Colonel Roosevelt stated:

"I spoke to the captain in command of the rear platoons (Dimmick), saying that I had been ordered to support the regulars in the attack upon the hills, and that in my judgment we could not take these hills by firing at them, and that we must rush them. He answered that his orders were to keep his men lying where they were, and that he could not charge without orders. I asked where the Colonel was, and as he was not in sight, said, 'Then I am the ranking officer here and I give the order to charge'—for I did not want to keep the men longer in the open, suffering under a fire which they could not effectively return. Naturally the captain hesitated to obey this order when no word had been received from his own Colonel. So I said, 'Then let my men through, sir,' and rode on through the lines, followed by the grinning Rough Riders, whose attention had been completely taken off the Spanish bullets, partly by my dialogue with the regulars, and partly by the language I had been using to themselves as I got the lines forward, for I had been joking with some and swearing at others, as the exigencies of the case seemed to demand. When we started to go through, however, it proved too much for the regulars, and they jumped up and came along, their officers and troops mingling with mine, all being delighted at the chance. When I got to where the head of the left wing of the Ninth was lying, through the courtesy of Lieutenant Hartwick, two of whose colored troopers threw down the fence, I was enabled to get back in the lane, at the same time waving my hat, and giving the order to charge the hill on our right front. Out of my sight, over on the right, Captains McBlaine and Taylor, of the Ninth, made up their minds independently to charge at just about this time; and at almost the same moment Colonels Carroll and Hamilton, who were off, I believe, to my left, where we could see neither them nor their men, gave the order to advance. But of all this I knew nothing at the time. The whole line, tired of waiting, and eager to close with the enemy, was straining to go forward; and it seems that different parts slipped the leash at almost the same moment. The First Cavalry came up the hill just behind, and partly mixed with my regiment and the Ninth."

In a letter to Captain Dimmick, dated July 31, 1898, Colonel Roosevelt stated:

"In response to my question, you told me that your colonel was further on. I recollect something being said about the brigade commander, which I did not understand. I replied that I had been ordered to support the 9th Cavalry in taking the hill ahead and that in my judgment we should take it by rushes. I said that as I was seemingly the highest officer there, I would take it upon myself to give the command to charge, which I accordingly did."

Captain Dimmick, in his official report, stated:

"Shortly after, the 1st Cavalry came up and formed on our left. Colonel Roosevelt of the 1st Volunteer Cavalry rode up, followed by some of his men in skirmish order. Colonel Roosevelt said, 'I understand the 9th Cavalry is carrying this hill by rushes and I am ordered to reinforce you. Where is your colonel?' Colonel Hamilton was then satisfying himself that the 1st Cavalry had formed on our left. At this point the order 'Forward' was given and *repeated to Colonel Roosevelt.* The line composed of Tutherly's squadron of the 1st Cavalry, Dimmick's squadron of the 9th Cavalry and Roosevelt's command of the 1st Volunteer Cavalry charged with a cheer and took the hill. Owing to the wire fences and dense undergrowth, the charge was one cheering mixed mass of the commands above mentioned."

Lieutenant Hartwick wrote to Colonel Roosevelt in August, explaining to him his error in assuming the credit of ordering the charge on San Juan Hill. Roosevelt replied as follows:

"Camp Wikoff, Montauk, Long Island
"August 27, 1898

"LIEUTENANT E. E. HARTWICK,
  "9TH CAVALRY, U. S. A.
"*Dear Lieutenant Hartwick:*
  "Your letter was most welcome and I fully appreciate the spirit in which you write. I remember you very well, and if you will permit me to say so, felt exceedingly glad to have so gallant a man near me in the battle.

"Frankly, your letter was the first intimation I had that I did not initiate the charge on the first hill. I never knew where Colonels Hamilton and Carroll were and am glad now to learn. In the confusion I had misunderstood matters and thought that they were on my left instead of my right. What you write makes me understand now for the first time how the charge was made. I did not know anyone else had ordered the charge. I was certainly up the hill first, and not knowing either of the colonels at that time I suppose

I failed to distinguish them. Understand me: I was merely up the hill first because I happened to have a horse. I entirely accept your statement and shall keep your letter so as to make matters perfectly plain and do full justice, when my article is written, to both the colonels. Evidently we charged independently at about the same time.

"I shall try to get over to your camp very soon.

"Very sincerely yours,
"THEODORE ROOSEVELT,
"*Colonel 1st U. S. V.*"

To this letter Lieutenant Hartwick attached the following notation:

"The above claim of Colonel Roosevelt is not true: in fact, the book he wrote, 'The Rough Riders,' proves this for he states that he had to dismount on account of the wire fence and tie his horse. This was done at the foot of the hill, whereas the rest of us ran up the hill without stopping. I also repeated the 'charge' to him."

In no way was the friendly acquaintanceship between Colonel Roosevelt and Lieutenant Hartwick affected by their differing views of the San Juan charge. Roosevelt mentioned Lieutenant Hartwick commendably in his published accounts and in after years, when they had occasion to meet during one of "Teddy's" campaign tours, nothing but the best fellowship prevailed, and after the death of Major Hartwick, Roosevelt was one of the first to write his sympathy.

Of the details of Lieutenant Hartwick's experiences in Cuba we can only refer to his diaries and letters appended to this sketch. The account of his adventures, the hardships he endured, the pleasures he enjoyed, and his description of the beauty and humor of life he found there is a tale of exceeding merit. Lieutenant Hartwick had the gift of expressing himself well.

The 9th Cavalry left Cuba August 14, 1898, upon the *U. S. S. Rio Grande* and was ordered to Camp Wikoff, Montauk Point, Long Island, where Lieutenant Hartwick remained until September, when he was transferred to Fort Huachuca, Arizona, with his command. In consideration of his services to the country and the military ability he had shown he was, on May 1, 1899, promoted from second to first lieutenant of cavalry.

Just before the departure of the troops from Cuba, a situation arose which made it necessary that either Lieutenant Hartwick or his bosom friend, Lieutenant Harry L. Cavenaugh, should remain while the other returned to the United States. Lieutenant John J. Pershing, now General Pershing, called at Hartwick's quarters and offered him his choice of going or remaining. It is probable that the hesitation to leave his comrade in Cuba was crowded from his mind by the thought of a certain picture he carried upon his person, but anyhow, Lieutenant Hartwick abandoned poor Cavenaugh to the heat of the tropics and ever afterward claimed that he was sorry for it. Lieutenant Cavenaugh was one of the closest friends possessed by Major Hartwick. He remained in the service and arose to the rank of brigadier-general. In the history of the recent World War the name of Harry LaTourette Cavenaugh occupies a high place, where his services in many of the major offensives as an officer in the 339th Division won for him a number of decorations for valor.

As stated in a subsequent paragraph, Lieutenant Hartwick was married October 19, 1898, and with his bride, returned to Huachuca. Life at a western army post in those days was not consonant with the ambitions of Lieutenant Hartwick, who desired to seek a vocation which should offer more activity and a greater field for his ability. Promotion was ahead, in fact, before he left the service he had passed the examinations for a captain's commission, but the utter monotony of post life, especially in comparison with the strenuous campaign which he had just undergone in Cuba, together with illness in his family which required his attention, caused him to offer his resignation to the war department. On July 8, 1898, the order was issued from the adjutant general's office, accepting his resignation in the name of the President, to take effect on August 31st following.

## Chapter II

Following his resignation from the army and a trip abroad with Mrs. Hartwick, Edward E. Hartwick returned to Grayling and for a time, or until he should decide as to the exact nature of his work in business, he held the position of cashier of the Bank of Grayling, this incumbency lasting from November, 1899, until April 1900.

The town of Grayling, where Mr. Hartwick passed his youth, was a lumber town, and the charm and interest of the lumber industry were in the atmosphere. Although this environment was a strong contributing factor to his selection of the lumber business as his life's work, Mr. Hartwick had never seriously studied the trade. He realized that although the business of the retail lumber trade offered a splendid return for successful effort, it was a business requiring undivided attention, hard labor, tedious detail, and that there was a large risk ever present. After due consideration of these things, he definitely decided to start, and in 1900 he purchased the interest of T. Hanson in the Hanson, Michelson Lumber Company, at Mason, Michigan, and the firm name was changed to the Hartwick, Michelson Lumber Company. Mason presented but a small field and in October, 1901, in company with Thomas Woodfield, Mr. Hartwick removed to Jackson, Michigan, where he assisted in the organization of the Hartwick-Woodfield Company, wholesale and retail dealers in lumber, millwork and fuel, also planing mill and dry kiln work. With a small beginning, this company quickly grew. The success of this company is but a commentary upon the business methods Mr. Hartwick introduced. Strict in the management of the work, he was yet a popular employer. As the son of his former partner wrote to him in after years: "My memory often takes me back to the days when you and my father came to Jackson and my early experiences as your office boy. In those days I used to think that you were too strict, and wondered if you ever remembered boyhood days. As I look back now and think of my need of education and the patience that you had with me and the willingness that you had in teaching me, it makes me feel that what little knowledge I now possess I owe mostly to you. Many times I express the hope that I can be as good a citizen and as well thought of as Mr. Hartwick and my father."

For eight years Mr. Hartwick acted as secretary and treasurer of the Hartwick-Woodfield Company at Jackson and, in fact, until his death in 1918, held an interest in the company. In addition to this business interest, while at Jackson, he was also president of the Corwin Lumber Company and of the Hartwick Machinery Company.

In 1909 Mr. Hartwick removed to Detroit and on January 20, 1909, launched the Hartwick Lumber Company, located at Clay Avenue and the Grand Trunk Railroad. This was an important step forward in his business career, but his success at Jackson gave him the necessary confidence to enlarge his field of activity and enter into competition with the largest companies of the state dealing in the retail lumber trade, with its allied interests. The company, as organized and so ably guided by Mr. Hartwick, steadily grew and the scope of the business now, which is conducted from five locations in the city of Detroit, is a just tribute to the founder. Mr. Hartwick's friends in the army believed that business had stolen an invaluable officer from the country, but his friends in civilian life naturally claimed the reverse. It is true that he was a born soldier, but his was a versatile character, and success seemed to have been foreordained in whatever vocation he might have adopted. Mr. Hartwick was also a director in the North Woodward Lumber Company of Detroit and the Radtke Lumber & Supply Company of Monroe, Michigan. A number of other important business and financial connections aside from the lumber trade were held by Mr. Hartwick. He was one of the first members of the Guaranty Trust Company of Detroit and was the first vice-president. He also promoted and served as director of the Michelson Land & Home Company and, upon the death of Frederick E. Michelson, who had been manager since its organization, Mr. Hartwick became manager.

The home life of Edward E. Hartwick closely approached the ideal. Married shortly after his return from Cuba to the sweetheart of his youth, he entered into a life of devotion and service to his wife and the splendid boys who came to him. The home and its duty to society was the chief interest of his life; the faithful companionship and loving co-operation with his wife was his greatest pleasure; and the rearing and education of his boys to clean manhood was his greatest ambition. At Grayling, Michigan, October 19, 1898, Edward E. Hartwick was married to Miss Karen Bessie Michelson, of that city, daughter of Nels and Margrethe (Jenson) Michelson. Her parents were natives of Denmark, and her father was one of the pioneers in the logging and lumber industry of that part of Michigan. Lieutenant Hartwick and his bride made their first home in the land of alkali and sagebrush, at Fort Huachuca, Arizona, and remained there for several months, or until Lieutenant Hartwick's resignation from the army. Those who were privileged to know Major Hartwick, recognized that the principal factor in his life, the stimulus of all his success and labor, was the thought of his family. Wherever he was, his mind naturally turned to their welfare. In France, whenever his duties permitted, he found his greatest recreation and rest in writing to his loved ones, "visiting" with them, as he termed it. In every beautiful scene, every interesting detail of life as he saw it, and in every day's work, there was something missing—the consciousness that they were not there to look with him upon those things and to share his experiences. Major and Mrs. Hartwick were the parents of three children: Edward Nelson, born May 3, 1903; Robert G., born May 5, 1906; and Edward Ernst, born June 13, 1911 and died December 10, 1912.

From France, six weeks before his death, Major Hartwick penned the following lines to his wife. These words, every one of which seemed divinely inspired, are from the open page of the man's heart. That the thoughts he expressed could not have been realized, challenges our reason, although there is provided the deathless heritage of his memory and the comforting knowledge that his desires are being fulfilled by others. Major Hartwick's letter, in part, follows:

"Some day I have dreamed that we shall see this country by auto together. For after this war and when I shall have been relieved from service with Uncle Samuel, I shall enter the service of companionship to you and incidentally be chum and instructor for the boys. To travel the rest of the world's path together, you and I; to guide our boys safely and successfully into their life work; to see them good men, strong morally as well as physically, so they may be a credit to themselves and their country and so to God and us—that, after this war, is my only ambition. So you may be making plans accordingly—not all idleness for me—some work—some recreation—books that for years I have been forced to neglect—music (?)—out-of-door life. And what shall the work be? Business with the boys as partners? Government work ties a fellow down and I am not to be chained down by business routine any more. What will the recreation be? Something we can enjoy together, and with the boys—travel, fishing trips, riding, dancing, golf, tennis—if music, I will be the listener. I suppose you will have it all planned when I get back."

In social life, at Grayling, at military stations, at Jackson, Detroit, or wherever he was known, Major Hartwick was most highly regarded and respected. He was one whose personality held exceeding charm, who was democratic and sympathetic with his fellows, and who was singularly appreciative of the qualities and weaknesses of his friends and associates. The men in the ranks honored him and took pleasure in obeying his orders, which they knew to be the most rigid law. He compelled strict obedience, but he fathered his men at the same time; he looked to their comfort and well-being before his own. In business circles he drew to himself friends by the score, such friends as many never have the good fortune to possess. His fraternal and club life may be indicated best by the names of the organizations to which he belonged. He was a 32d degree Mason, having been a member of Jackson Lodge, No. 17, F. & A. M., Jackson Chapter, No. 3, R. A. M., Detroit Commandery, No. 1, K. T., Moslem Temple, A. A. O. N. M. S., of Detroit, and the Michigan Sovereign Consistory, Valley of Detroit, Michigan. Major Hartwick's clubs were: the Detroit Athletic Club, the Ingleside Club, Detroit Golf Club, Bankers' Club of Detroit, Fellowcraft Athletic Club, and the Detroit Automobile Club. He held membership with the National Association of Real Estate Exchanges, Detroit Real Estate Board, Detroit Board of Commerce, Detroit Real Estate Exchange, Exchange Club, Detroit Y. M. C. A., American National Red Cross, Detroit Retail Lumber Dealers' Association, Milwaukee Junction Manufacturers' Association, and was president and director of the Michigan State Retailers' Lumber Association.

In religious matters Major Hartwick believed in God and His guidance. From Cuba he wrote, to his future bride:

"When we charged up the hill I gave myself to my God, so I didn't think of dying, except that I didn't think I would get up alive. But thank Him that he spared me. I write you this because you asked if I were afraid to meet my God. No, life is sweet and I want to return to you, but if God wills it different, may He help me always to do my duty."

Major Hartwick lived his religion, rather than acted it, He was not sectarian or biased in his views upon questions of theology and he respected the other man's religion as well as his own. That "many roads lead to Rome" expresses his belief, for if good was achieved the method was immaterial. Major Hartwick attended the North Woodward Congregational Church.

Politically, Major Hartwick never had aspiration to hold public office, although he did serve at one time in Jackson as police commissioner. Nominally, the major was a republican and a strong supporter of that party at the polls, but he believed in good government and loyalty to the administration whether it was republican or democratic. For those forces which would destroy the unity of government and wreck civilization through ignorance and greed, Major Hartwick held nothing but contempt and hostility. The ideals of which the symbol is the red flag were inexorably opposed by him. His experience in the service of the United States taught him that nothing was so efficacious in treating with such influences as the employment of force. Major Hartwick's experience had also shown him that the best preparation for peace was preparation for war. Although believing that thorough preparedness was the best preventive of war, had he lived to see the inauguration of the great world movements for the promotion of peace, he would have supported them had he perceived in them the least sign of practicability. In local matters and in those things which tended to national, state or civic improvement, Major Hartwick was an earnest and enthusiastic worker. Good roads, proper utilization of land and resources, conservation of timber, and other topics of economic interest, are treated by him in the personal papers with which, very fortunately, we have been able to supplement this biography.

When the United States entered the war against Germany in April, 1917, Edward E. Hartwick experienced an overpowering call to the colors. The soldier in him came to the front and he immediately set about devising a way to re-enter the service. In fact, before Congress and President Wilson declared a state of war in existence, he wrote to his old comrade, Maj. Kenzie W. Walker, who was attached to the quartermaster general's office, stating that he desired to offer his services. From that time on he held a steady correspondence with the secretary of war, the quartermaster general of the army, Congressman Doremus, Senator Townsend, Howard E. Coffin, who was secretary of the National Council of Defense, the Michigan War Preparedness Board, the adjutant general of the U. S. Army, and many others, seeking an entrance to the active service of his country. He reiterated in every letter his reasons for wishing to go into the service again, his experience, his wish to place this training at the disposal of others, and the belief that it was his solemn duty to offer himself. Response to his inquiries and requests was at first discouraging, and for a time it appeared that, notwithstanding his former army experience, he would not succeed in finding a place. Major Hartwick was then a man of forty-five years of age, although a much younger man physically, but the processes of government were slow, especially during that later war period when everything was much in a state of disorganization.

At length, an appointment became a possibility and on September 6, 1917, he was commissioned a major of engineers of the officers' reserve corps. The forestry service of this corps was then being established and trained, and on September 11th Major Hartwick received a telegram from Adjutant General McCain to report immediately to the commanding officer of the 20th Engineers at Camp American University, on the outskirts of Washington, D. C.

It may be remarked in passing that the forestry service was one of the most important branches of the United States Army. The necessity of timber in tremendous quantities was constant, and the allied leaders looked to the United States to contribute materially to the forces engaged in supplying this timber. Wood was needed in the construction of dugouts, trenches, barracks, hospitals, roads, walks, camouflage screens, bridges, etc. The need may be better emphasized by the statement that one French Army Corps utilized 30,000 trees in one day alone. The 20th Engineers (Forestry) was under the command of Col. W. A. Mitchell, U. S. A. The personnel of the ranks was of foresters, woodsmen, and sawmill workers; each battalion contained three companies of 250 men each, and there were designed to be ten battalions, with an additional nine service battalions, thus making a regiment of over 17,000 men, the largest in the world.

Major Hartwick was given command of the 1st Battalion at Camp American University and immediately began to instruct his men in the rudiments of warfare. Time was short and a protracted training period was impossible, consequently the routine was one of severe attention to the task in hand. The work of organization proceeded rapidly as the time for embarkation was expected to come any moment. In order to be near his family until the last moment before departing, Major Hartwick had secured a home for Mrs. Hartwick and his two sons in Washington, just a few miles from the camp. September passed, then October. At dusk on Sunday evening, November 11th, just one year before the armistice was signed, the engineers marched out of Camp American University. The 1st and 2nd Battalions were placed on board the U. S. Transport *Madawaska*, formerly the German liner *König Wilhelm II*, and on the 12th the boat sailed from its port, New York City, for France.

Then followed the voyage through the submarine-infested sea, the arrival at St. Nazaire, the debarkation there, and finally the transfer to Dax, where Major Hartwick was stationed with his staff during his entire time in France. It would be presumptuous to describe in detail these experiences, when we have such a realistic pen picture of his own, in the form of a diary journal which he kept from day to day. No better commentary upon the thorough instruction and training Major Hartwick had given his command in the comparatively short space of two months may be given than the formal statement of the commander of the *Madawaska*, presented to Major Hartwick shortly before their arrival at St. Nazaire:

"So noteworthy has been the conduct, discipline and bearing of the troops under your command while embarked in this vessel, that it calls for some expression from me, as Commanding Officer of the ship.

"Your men have distinguished themselves by orderly quietness and promptness at abandon ship drill and at all other times; by keeping their quarters, washrooms and latrines scrupulously clean, and by standing an earnest, interested and excellent lookout.

"They have won the admiration and liking of the officers and men of this ship who have been proud and glad to be associated with them, and feel sure that in the future they will render an excellent account of themselves.
"Edward Watson."

Another compliment was received by Major Hartwick just after the removal of his command from St. Nazaire to Dax. This follows:

"Camp Headquarters, Base Section No. 1—France
"Headquarters 20th Engineers in France
"From Camp Commander,
"To Maj. E. E. Hartwick, Commanding 20th Engineers
"My dear Major:
"Allow me to express to you and to your officers and men my appreciation of excellent discipline displayed by your command and the good conduct which characterized it while in this camp. Notwithstanding the heavy details of men for building dams and other important engineer work, you have been able to improve the barracks and grounds which you occupied. I inspected your barracks after your regiment left and found all property in excellent condition and properly cared for and the grounds in the vicinity well policed. Every effort seems to have been made by your command to leave everything in better shape than it was when you arrived. For this reason we look upon your stay with us as a blessing which I am sorry has not been the case with a number of organizations.
"You may well feel that you have helped us along in our great work here instead of retarding us.
"My best wishes go with you and all of the other officers and men of the Twentieth Engineers.
"Yours sincerely,
"N. F. McClure,
"Colonel 22nd Cavalry, Commanding."

This latter commendation was made a part of a general letter to all organizations later, citing how well a command could behave and as an example for them to emulate.

Major Hartwick and his men were delayed in beginning the actual operation of sawing lumber by the failure of the American mills to arrive. Each battalion was supposed to have had a complete outfit for logging and sawmill operations. Small mills were purchased from the French, however, and regular work was done until the arrival of the American machinery in March of 1918. The 20th also laid many miles of railroad track and sidings for troop trains. Shortly before his death Major Hartwick was engaged in the construction of ice-houses, the largest for the manufacture and storing of ice in the history of the industry. The lumber for these was taken by the engineers from a fifty-year-old forest.

Of the regular day to day life of these engineers, their work and their play, we have many intimate glimpses from the journal of Major Hartwick. Major Hartwick devised every scheme possible for the benefit of his men, the occupation of their time and their protection in a strange country with different customs. He believed that, were not healthful recreation provided for the men at their camp, they would seek it elsewhere, to their own danger. Carl G. Doney, president of Willamette University, of Salem, Oregon, then engaged in Y. M. C. A. work overseas, wrote as follows to Mrs. Hartwick:

"March 4, 1918

"Mrs. Edward E. Hartwick,
"Detroit, Mich.
"*Dear Mrs. Hartwick:*
"This letter is from one who is a stranger to you and who writes simply because he has had the fine privilege of meeting your husband, his officers and men during a stay of three days in the camp.

"I left a wife and two lads in the States and know something of the anxiety and questionings in their minds, know that much of this is the reaction of imaginings and know also that they do not quite believe I tell them the whole truth about my condition here. For these reasons I requested and secured the consent of your husband to write to you, but he will not see this letter and will not know its contents.

"I am here giving addresses to the men and have been able to learn much that might be denied to others. At the Y. M. C. A. headquarters I first heard of the outstanding record made by the Major and his men, for months the best moral and disciplinary achievement of any in the entire base section. Dr. Exner, who studied the army conditions on the Mexican border, says in his report that the officer in command of soldiers is responsible to the extent of at least seventy-five percent for their goodness or badness.

"Coming to this place, I was prepared to find an excellent situation, but everything is better than was anticipated. The camps are delightfully and healthfully located, the quarters of the officers and men are so comfortable that one wishes to remain. The food is better than we had in the States, well served and of wide variety.

"The devotion of the men to the Major is almost touching; one private saying to me, 'There is not a man in all of these companies who would not die in his tracks for the Major.' This is quite in contrast to what I have found elsewhere. All of these men have loved ones who are anxiously concerned for their welfare. I wish they might know the man who looks after them, might know how he has protected them and given them an *esprit de corps* which will bring them home again better than when they left.

"This letter, therefore, is just to tell you these things and to express the judgment that your sacrifice is meaning everything to the men here and to their waiting loved ones in America. It may be an unheralded service, but it is none the less beautiful and essential in its results over here. The knowledge of your contribution to the great cause may make it a little easier to bear the trial of separation. And perhaps I should add that the work being done here by the men is so extensive and important that there appears to be little probability that they will ever be near the front or see any danger.

"Please pardon my presumption in thus addressing you and let my good intentions be its justification.

"Very respectfully,
"CARL G. DONEY."

One of the chief entertainments provided for his "boys" by Major Hartwick was an athletic festival for Washington's Birthday of 1918. In addition to his account in his own journal, he wrote as follows to his son, Nelson:

"We invited the public in general and then, by our request, the French military *commandante* submitted to us a list of French notables—military and civil—that we should invite in addition to our own personal friends among the people here. His list started with the *sou-prefet* (lieutenant-governor) and included the chief military surgeon, the mayors and under-mayors of this town and adjoining towns, the head of the French Red Cross, postmasters, invalided French officers here and their families, if they have any.

"He also suggested that we advertise it in the papers and send the editors invitations. So we asked him to do it for us, and he even had notices of the meet in papers 100 miles distant. So our especially invited French guests numbered more than 300. This was in addition to our own visiting American officers, their band, ball teams and the Canadian officers. It meant we furnished refreshments for that crowd and in addition conveyed them to and from the scene of athletic contention. Well, we did it all right. We fed them on lettuce and beef sandwiches, doughnuts, tarts, cake, apple pie and washed it down with punch and coffee.

"The invited French filled one grandstand to capacity. It was lucky we had the athletic field roped off with sentinels and bayoneted guns to police it. The visitors, including uninvited, numbered more than 4,000 all told. It was some feat to make our refreshments satisfy all hands. But it was a great afternoon, the two bands furnishing plenty of music and finishing with the two national airs, 'Star Spangled Banner' and the 'Marseillaise,' during which the whole crowd stood with bared heads and afterwards cheered mightily. But our trial came after the show, for we had but six trucks and three Fords to get the invited guests home, while the uninvited attempted to pile in also. I rode to my quarters in a Canadian major's auto and the trip reminded me of traveling to a football game at Ann Arbor."

*La Petite Voix*, the official paper of the 20th Engineers, in speaking of the occasion, stated:

"In behalf of the entire company, *La Petite Voix* thanks Major Hartwick for his commendation of our behavior last Sunday. We feel proud of the compliment and shall endeavor to merit a bigger one at the next occasion of such a nature."

Of the death of Major Hartwick, little can be added to the accounts given by his brother officers who were with him at the last. One of the last letters received in Detroit was written by the major just five days before he breathed his last; this was addressed to Mr. C. M. Burton, and a portion of it follows:

"Words of mine are not sufficient to tell you how pleased I was to receive your letter of February 6th, received here March 23rd. I hope I appreciate your taking the time from your business to write me and also that you put it in longhand. I would prefer to write this to you in the same manner were I not today, by the direction of the doctor, ordered under the blankets with the hope that I may get out of bed in two days. These last ten days I have been working very hard and did not realize my limitations until I was 'all in.' This is the first time I have been on 'sick report' in all my previous eleven years' service with Uncle Sam's regulars, but I suppose I have to realize that I am not so young as I was then and that if 'youth cannot be denied, age will tell.' I caught a hard cold about ten days ago, but kept plugging along until it developed into la grippe, so I should be out in a couple of days."

Major Hartwick's death occurred Sunday, March 31, 1918, at 3:25 p. m. (French time) and he was buried at Bordeaux at 3 p. m. Monday. Under the date of April 2d, Capt. L. M. Pill, of the Engineers, Major Hartwick's adjutant, wrote the following letter:

"*Dear Mrs. Hartwick:*

"The last few days have been the saddest days in my life, for my commander and my very dear friend has gone. I know that nothing I can say can lessen the grief you feel, but I know it will be a comfort to you to know how he died and when and how he was buried.

"The Major had been complaining of having a cold for ten days or two weeks previous to the time when he was taken ill, but this had apparently left him and on Sunday, March 24th, seemed to me to be particularly bright and in excellent spirits. After supper Sunday night he left the camp, saying he was going to take a walk. Monday morning he didn't come over to breakfast and about 9 o'clock I went to the hotel where he stayed and found him in the sitting room, wrapped up in his overcoat and feeling very badly. He said he thought he would go to bed for the day, as he thought he had the grippe, as he ached all over and was sore in his chest. As soon as the doctor returned (he was at that time at one of the companies), about 10 o'clock, he had the Major go to bed and sent one of his men, Private John Gude, who had been acting as the Major's orderly, to wait on him. Up to that time no symptoms of the disease had appeared and we all thought the Major had a slight attack of the grippe. That day the regimental surgeon, Captain Houle, arrived, and in the afternoon he and I went over to see the Major, whom we found feeling very much better. He told us that he was feeling so much better that he was only staying in bed because the doctor had so ordered. We had planned to have a dinner Tuesday night in honor of a couple of French officers whom the Major esteemed very highly, and he instructed us to complete the plans as he would be able to attend. That night (Monday) he dictated to Sergeant Coleman the letters I sent to you unsigned.

"Sometime in the night—I think about 3 o'clock—he awoke in violent pain and sent for the medical officer, Lieutenant Aldrich, who, upon his arrival, found him in a stupor. He was immediately removed to the French Hospital here and the case was diagnosed as cerebro-spinal meningitis. The serum was immediately administered and the French medical officers called into consultation. These officers agreed with our officers as to the nature of the disease and method of treatment and assumed charge of the case. A few days later Colonel Shaw came down, bringing with him Lieutenant Binger* of the medical corps, who was a specialist in this disease. Lieutenant Binger was with the Major night and day until he died, and everything that could possibly be done was done, but he at no time fully recovered consciousness. I was in his room a few moments before he died and I know that he did not suffer. I don't think he felt any pain after he was first stricken. The care and sympathy of the French officers, Captains Boucoud and Beaumont, and of the French nurse, Sister Marthe, was wonderful. I know it will be a source of comfort to you, as it was to all of us who loved him, to know that he had this care in this foreign land.

"The Major had known since we first arrived here a French soldier priest, L'Abbi Jb. Emmanuel Combi, who had lived in England and therefore spoke English. This Catholic Father is attached to the office of the Chef de Medicin, and as soon as he heard of the Major's illness went at once to the hospital, and was there every day until the end. He placed himself absolutely at our service and this assistance was invaluable. The Major was genuinely loved by the people with whom he came in contact over here and the whole town was shocked when he died.

"We took him to Bordeaux and buried him on Monday at 3

*Dr. Carl Binger, of the Massachusetts Base Hospital, organized in Boston.

o'clock in the Talence Cemetery. The commanding general furnished an escort of a battalion of infantry and he was buried with full military honors. The French general commanding this region sent a number of his staff officers, and France and our own country again joined hands over the grave of a noble soldier. I have had some pictures taken of the grave and will send you some of the flowers. The rose leaves were handed to me by an old, gray Mother of France, whose sons had died, as our Major died, for Freedom. I have asked the commanding general for permission to send you the flag that flew in front of his tent and that was used to cover the casket at the funeral.

"The Major was one of the best friends I have ever had and it was a great privilege to have known him. He was beloved by all the officers and men of this battalion. I have never known a man more devoted to his family. Before this war is over, America will have given many of her sons to Freedom, but no truer soldier or nobler man than my commander. He will always be 'Our Major' to the officers and men of this battalion."

## In a later letter, Captain Pill wrote:

"All the men loved, respected and admired him and had he lived he would have attained high rank in the A. E. F. Colonel Mitchell has often said to me, 'What a pity Major Hartwick had to be taken and what a misfortune. He should have been colonel of the 20th.' I have never met an officer over here, and as you can imagine I have met a number, who took such an interest in the welfare of his men and his officers and who was so thoroughly competent to look after them."

## From Lieutenant John B. Cuno, of the 20th, there came the following communication regarding Major Hartwick:

"While the coals are still glowing and the thing is fresh in my memory, and also fearing that in the rush and bustle of affairs in this great war it may be overlooked by others, I want to give you a little account of our dear Major's funeral. I am stationed in the large city north of where the battalion is located (Bordeaux) and had seen the Major just a few days ago when he was up here on business. He had come up to meet an incoming detachment of the 20th Engineers and to look after them. He had already found straw and dry wood and good camp grounds for them at their destination, but had come up to see that they got their rations and more tentage, because they had brought with them only five days' rations and their pup tents. I remember so well how he urged the quartermaster to furnish the tentage and how he obtained the five days' rations for the detachment, and how he even borrowed a truck to send them a distance of over 96 miles. He certainly made me step around and do some work when he was with me those few days (in army language 'he was on my tail all the time'). At the time he left to go back to Dax he had a bad cold, but I never thought anything of it. In a few days you can imagine how surprising it was to receive word that he had contracted meningitis. Think of it, the only case in our battalion which was fifty miles from any other troops, and for it to take hold of our leader. News of its seriousness came, and also that everything possible was being done for him, but at that it was a shock to hear of his passing away on March 31st. It was hard to believe. Just ten days ago I had invited him to eat supper with me in my little boarding house, and had been traveling around in the city with him on business which he now and then interrupted to snap a few pictures. He took some of the monuments and fountains and buildings in town, and I took one of him standing before a statue of Gambetta. He told me about how his boy had sent him the pocket camera and wanted him to be sure and take 'lots of pictures.' Yes, it is hard to realize that he has left us, especially those who were near him every day in his work. He only saw me occasionally, but I always thought so much of him.

"I recall one windy, black night coming over on the transport, when he was walking up and down on the hurricane deck for exercise. I happened to run into him and he said to me in such a fatherly way, 'Well, how are you tonight?' Another time I remember him saying, as we entered the French port in the glory of a beautiful day, 'Oh, if my wife were only here to enjoy this scenery with me.' Those little things always stuck with me, the fact that he was such a home-like man who so loved his dear ones he had left behind.

"But I meant this to be short, just to say a word about the funeral, just to say what a bright, clear, sunny day it was, and how the infantry battalion, headed by its band playing the funeral march, led out from the base hospital to the little cemetery some half-mile away, and how the officers and men of the 20th followed in the procession. It was such a simple, brief affair, and the warm-hearted French folk gathered quietly in the cemetery to attend the ceremony. The firing-squad did its work, and we turned and left the place which will not be forgotten by any of us."

From a man in the ranks, Private M. F. Malone, came these words:

"I am only a private, but having been in the office with and around the Major since the organization of his battalion in Washington, I naturally came to know him and I consider it not only an honor, but a revelation, to have been associated with and commanded by a man of his character and ability. He was never-tiring in his labors, never-weakening in his undertakings, and always looking out for the comfort and welfare of his men. He was faithful to his country, he was faithful to his family, and thus he came to the end of a perfect day on this earth. And now I would write across his records 'here was a MAN and a SOLDIER to the end.'"

Upon the very day of his death there appeared in *La Petite Voix* an Easter greeting from Major Hartwick to the men of the 1st Battalion, 20th Engineers. He wrote:

"It is appreciated as an honor to be asked to 'write something' for *La Petite Voix* and it is regretted by the writer that his pen cannot produce something really worthy of the invitation and the space offered. It is understood that the space will be in your 'Easter Number' and so what is written should be apropos.

"Easter morning being the anniversary of the resurrection of Our Saviour we are reminded that whether in conformation of the universal plan of the Almighty Father, or merely by chance, it is a fact that this anniversary comes at a season most appropriate of all the seasons of the year,—at a time when all vegetation that was *seemingly* killed by the frosts and cold of Autumn and buried in the snows and ice of Winter, is being resurrected, born anew and putting forth new life to sustain and nourish the children of the earth, a parallel with the life, death and resurrection of Our Lord Jesus Christ, who after *seeming* death was buried, but arose from the grave to sustain and nourish our faith in Him and in the immortality of the soul.

"For as, locally in this district, this season and our surroundings I am sure will remind us that Providence has favored us and been especially kind. We have an unusually healthy camping ground and surroundings, plenty of all the necessities and many of the comforts, all of which should impress on us that it is our duty not only to our country but to our God, to not thoughtlessly accept all these blessings, but to endeavor to use them so as to keep both our bodies and our spirits as nearly as possible in harmony with the example given us by Him, the anniversary of whose resurrection is so near at hand, and in so doing not only to perform our duty to our country, but actually live our gratitude to our Saviour."

The issue of *La Petite Voix* of April 6th was headed: "This Issue of *La Petite Voix* is dedicated to the memory of our late commander, Major Edward E. Hartwick." The front page of the paper bore the following announcement:

"THE LAST TAPS IS SOUNDED
FOR MAJOR HARTWICK

"Last Sunday afternoon the Angel of Death took from us our esteemed Commander, Major Edward E. Hartwick. Major Hartwick was sick less than week. Two weeks ago he came out to Company C and personally delivered to the editor an article expressing his greetings to the men of the First Battalion. It appeared in last week's Easter issue.

"That beautiful acknowledgment of his deep faith in our Saviour was the last public message he wrote. The touching sincerity, now that he is gone, seems to vaguely reveal a knowledge that something was going to happen.

"Two days before the Major became ill, he requested some of the boys who were playing near his office not to swear, saying, 'Boys, I wish you wouldn't profane so much. You can't tell when you might be called from this life; and I'd hate for any of you boys to die so unprepared.'

"This little incident is characteristic of the Major. He was profoundly devoted to his family. Next to that came his country's interests, in which he was engaged at the time of his death. A tireless worker to the end, his mind was constantly on his duties.

"Major Hartwick, after graduating from West Point Military Academy and serving several years in the Service, went into business in Detroit, Michigan, and at the time of his death was president of the Hartwick Lumber Company and first vice-president of the Guaranty Trust Company, both of that city. He was a very successful business man, and when the United States entered the war, he gave up his many obligations at home and rallied to the call of his country. He had served her well—and paid the supreme price of patriotism—his life."

In the same issue of *La Petite Voix* appeared the following:

### "A Tribute by John F. McNichol, Company A

"It was with feelings of sincere sorrow that we heard, on Easter Sunday, of the passing to the great beyond of Major Edward E. Hartwick, 1st Battalion, 20th Engineers.

"It was on a Sunday, but a few weeks ago, that he so impressed us with an address on 'Father's Day.' The memory of his words still linger in our minds. He told us in a very impressive manner, of his own experience on 'Father's Day' back home. His few well chosen words could not but help to sink deep and they created a 'Dad, I am proud of you' feeling among his audience.

"His contribution to the Easter edition of *La Petite Voix* speaks for itself. His message brings out his character as a soldier and a man. Little did he think that he would not be able to read it in print, but such is the uncertainty of time.

"His loss is great, not only to his immediate family, but equally to his battalion and regiment. What greater love can a man show, than to lay down his life for his country and his fellowmen?

"In conclusion, we can best express ourselves by the following quotation by Fitz James Halleck:

> "*'Green be the turf above you,*
> *Friend of my better days;*
> *None knew thee, but to love you,*
> *Nor names thee, but to praise.*
> *Tears fell when thou we'rt dying,*
> *From eyes unused to weep.*
> *And long where thou art lying*
> *Will tears, the cold earth steep.'*"

Editorially, *La Petite Voix* stated:

"When the news reached the men of Companies A, C, and Headquarters that Major Hartwick had passed away, it cast a pall of sorrow over the camps.

"The Major had won the profound respect of every man under his command because he possessed that acumen, which is an essence of greatness, to see and understand the position of every soldier regardless of how menial his labor or how humble his station.

"His personal interests were subordinated to those of his country and fellowmen.

"Every human being has an individuality, but few have what Major Hartwick possessed, a strong personality. He was tender-hearted and sympathetic; strong-willed and influential. His deep love for home ties marks him as the type of American fatherhood that has elevated us to the foremost position of the world in the Christianity of the hearthstone.

"The writer remembers the eventful night that this battalion, just at dusk, marched quietly out of Camp American University on our way to France. The Major's wife and children were sitting in an automobile. When he kissed his little boy good-bye, the little fellow shook with sobs. He did not realize that that was the last time he would ever see his Daddy again. Many are the homes that will be depleted by this war, but may the great God that we all worship grant that the end will justify the prodigious cost. In years to come we will glance through the shadowy realm of memory and recall the kindness and devotion that distinguished real MEN from their likenesses that only move in an individual sphere. We mourn the loss of a man who was taken at a time when his country most needed him."

An affectionate tribute was accorded Major Hartwick in the columns of *L'Avenir Republicain*, Dax, France, issue of April 14, 1918. The translation of the original French follows:

"Sunday afternoon, Easter Day, Major Edward E. Hartwick

died at the military hospital in our town. Forty-six years of age, in the fullness of his physical and intellectual powers, he has been taken in a few days by an all-destroying disease.

"Destiny did not will that this veteran of the Cuban War, this former Lieutenant of Captain Pershing, commander-in-chief today of the Americans in France, should be killed by the enemy he had come so far to seek and whom he always desired to encounter.

"He has found death in the midst of his many daily duties, in the accomplishment of an important task which was given him by his chiefs for the common good. He has none the less fallen, in the full meaning of the word, a brave and loyal soldier of the Right. His loss is profoundly felt at Dax, where his goodness, his affability, and his smiling courtesy had conquered all sympathies for him—sympathies which were dear to him, we know.

"All are united in this sad circumstance in addressing to Major Hartwick the homage of a last adieu; to his companions in arms the expression of their condolences.

"They pray more particularly that Captain Pill and Lieutenant Freedman, the immediate collaborators of our missing ally and friend, will be good enough to be their interpreters to Mrs. Hartwick and to his dear children.

"They would have them tell, in the name of all of us, how much we share in their sorrow and with what fidelity the memory of their husband and father will be guarded in this little corner of France, where he died for the immortal cause that unites our two countries."

The following transcription is self-explanatory:

"Headquarters, 20th Engineers, N. A. U. S. M. P. O., No. 717, A. E. F., 31, March, '18
"Regimental Special Order⎫
Number 2                        ⎭

"1. It is with deep regret that the Commanding Officer announces the death of Major Edward E. Hartwick in Dax, Landes, at three twenty-five p. m., today, of cerebro-spinal meningitis.

"2. Major Hartwick was a graduate of West Point and for several years an officer of cavalry in the United States Army. He resigned during the period of peace, and engaged in the lumber business, where he promptly rose to prominence. At the time of the declaration of war against Germany he was president of the Hartwick Lumber Company, Detroit, Michigan, but he put aside personal interests in order to serve his country, and accepted a commission as Major of the 1st Battalion, 20th Engineers.

"3. Major Hartwick possessed in an unusual degree the qualities needed by the officers and soldiers of the United States Army. He was patriotic and loyal to the extreme, steadfast in his devotion to duty, capable and energetic at all times, and his personal example was always an encouragement to his men.

"4. In these times when hearts are tried, strength is tested, and lives are lost, it is expected that many of us will follow him in death, and we must all try to serve our country as well and faithfully as he had done.

"5. Commanding Officers of all Companies and Detachments of the 20th Engineers will assemble their troops at 4 p. m. Saturday, April 6th, and personally read this order to them.

"W. A. MITCHELL,
"*Colonel, 20th Engineers, N. A., Commanding.*"

From Colonel Mitchell himself came the following letter to Mrs. Hartwick:

"Like lightning from a clear sky, came the telegram that Major Hartwick was very sick, and then that he had died. Only a few days before, I had been with him and we had renewed our friendship of American University, and he was well and happy.

"He was the same man in France as he was in the United States, doing his duty cheerfully and in the best possible manner.

"His loss is personal and official. The regiment feels and mourns his loss, and I feel and mourn his loss, and we all know that our loss is only a small one compared to yours.

"The Major was well, or fairly well, in the evening, but was suddenly taken ill in the night and lost consciousness soon thereafter. He practically never recovered consciousness and it is some comfort to know that he never suffered and that death was painless. He was buried in Bordeaux, with military honors.

"It is hard, but it must be borne. Providence moves in a mysterious way, and Major Hartwick did his best, and we are all doing our best. As I see it, your best will be very well done if you can bring up each of his two sons to be anything like the man that their father was.

"Inclosed I send you a copy of an order that was published to the regiment. It was a small thing for so great a loss, but it was all that I could do. May the Lord bless you and help you to bear up in your distress."

That the French people with whom Major Hartwick had been associated felt profoundly the loss of their friend is shown by the expressions written by them. Noteworthy among these are the ones presented below:

"April the 1st, 1918
"Sir:
"I have heard with great sorrow of the death in the field of Major Hartwick and in my own name and in the name of the French Army which I represent I wish to convey to you our sympathy in the loss which you and the American Army have suffered.

"Should an opportunity arise I would ask you to be so kind as to tender our condolences to the deceased's wife and family and tell them, that we, French people, fully appreciate the value of the sacrifice which this American officer made for our cause by laying down his life.

"I am, sir,
"Yours very respectfully,
E. Camille Grevosh,
*Interpreter to the British Army, G. H. Q.
(C. F. C.-Dax)*"

"Madame:
"At last I got your address and, although very late, my husband and I feel that we have to send you the expression of our deep and sincere condolences.

"We were very happy to receive Commander Hartwick, for whom we felt a real sympathy. The sight of our children seemed to take away all his preoccupations, and he was delighted to talk about you and his sons. I saw him on Thursday before his death and there was nothing to foretell so rapid an end; he only seemed very sad to be so far away from you and the children. According to meager information, he was struck before knowing it. The commander has left at Dax nothing but regrets, not only among the civilians, but among his officers and soldiers. Everyone was dismayed. I assure you, Madame, we have been very deeply depressed. M. Boulart wishes his respectful regards sent to you, and you may be assured of all my sympathies. We are at your entire disposal for any service or pleasure we can give you.

"M. Boulart."

(Translation)

"Dax, le 22 April, 1918

"Madame:
"If there are sorrows which one respects by silence, nevertheless it seems a way is pointed out for the souls which meet each other in God. In your misfortune, allow me to show my sympathy in speaking of your dear departed one who, with my family, I saw almost till his last moments. The Major had told you our house, where he had been installed since his arrival in Dax—had become a little his, for we had so begged him to so consider it. After his day's work was all finished—for above all he was the slave to duty—he relaxed in coming to pass his evenings with us, and with me he worked at French with a rare energy. I was proud of the progress of my pupil which permitted us to talk lengthily of you, Madame, and of your sons. His last evenings above all, it seems to me, were filled with reminiscences of you. This perfect model of the head of a family has left among us a too sympathetic regret for our thoughts not to turn to you in the hour of your affliction, for our hearts not to assure you of our share in your sorrow.

"The Major was suddenly taken ill while with us—we thought with a simple chill, but which the doctors judged more serious and suddenly removed him. Every day I went to the hospital, where he was perfectly cared for, to ask for news of him of the sister who never left him. No care or devotion was spared, whether by his men, by whom he was deeply loved, or by the doctors who cared for him as a brother, but the Great Master had decided. What can we do before Him and what can we ask Him in your behalf, if not the courage He gives great souls!

"Immediately after the Major's arrival at the hospital, I carried to the sister who nursed him a little medal of the Holy Virgin. She put it under his head and this last souvenir, which did not leave him till after his death, goes to you. I send it, Madame, with the hope that it will reach you safely.

"The soul of him who has departed will watch over you—over his dear ones, for you know that all is not ended here below, but on the contrary all lives in the spirit and there remains to us all efficacious means to show our dead the fidelity of our remembrance in the strength of our prayers. This assurance will be for you, dear Madame, an alleviation to your sorrow, which I entrust to God! The more cruel the trial, the nearer we must be to Him who crushes, but always supports us!

"The too short stay of the Major near us has left profound regrets. I express them to you in my name and that of my family, in begging you to accept the expression of our deepest sentiments of sympathy.
"MARIE CASENAVE.

"I have asked a friend to translate my letter, written in French, as I have not yet made sufficient progress in English to write myself, so it is through her, Madame, that I can send this letter."

From Theodore Roosevelt, whose own hour was but a few months removed, there came a brief expression of esteem, as follows:

"April 16, 1918
"My dear Mrs. Hartwick:
"I have learned with genuine concern of the death of your gallant husband. His going to the war as he did was entirely characteristic of him. These are very hard days for all of us. One of my own sons has been grievously wounded; and at least I can assure you of my most heartfelt sympathy.
"Very respectfully yours,
THEODORE ROOSEVELT."

These published letters are but a few of the many which were forthcoming after Major Hartwick's death. From his friends in the army, in business, and whose lives had somewhere touched his, there came a universal expression

Lieutenant Edward E. Hartwick in 1898. This picture, made by a Santiago photographer shortly after the capture of the city by the American troops, shows the lieutenant mounted upon a captured Spanish cavalry pony

of genuine sorrow. Associations with which the Major had been connected drafted resolutions in his memory and from companies and individuals in his own vocation, the lumber trade, there came letters from every part of the country. Little more can be added to the story of this man's career. His mortal remains were removed from Bordeaux to Detroit in the late weeks of 1920 and upon December 23d were laid to rest in Woodlawn Cemetery. In October, 1921, a beautiful stone and bronze memorial, surmounting an underground mausoleum, was placed in position upon an elevated portion of Woodlawn. As an artistic conception, this memorial is matchless, and as a type of memorial architecture it is distinctive and impressive. Upon the large bronze bas-relief, placed in harmonious relation to the classic stone work, is represented a full-length figure of a major of engineers, standing before the grave of a French poilu, beside him the figures of two orphaned French children, over whom he has assumed protection. The eyes of the officer are turned toward the setting sun, perceiving in the beautiful coloration a forecast, a spiritual prophecy of the peace and happiness which will follow the death and desolation of war; but the eyes of the two little orphans, turned toward the little mound and cross before them, see only the sorrow and loss embodied in the grave of their parent. The scene is truly symbolical of the man whom it memorializes. In lasting metal the lines from Markham, which follow, are inscribed.

> "They are not dead; life's flag is never furled;
>   They passed from world to world.
> Their bodies sleep, but in some nobler land
>   Their spirits march under a new command.
> New joys await them there,
>   In hero-heavens, wrapt in immortal air.
>
> "How shall we honor their deed—
>   How speak our praise of this immortal breed?
> Only by living nobly as they died—
>   Toiling for truth denied,
> Loyal to something bigger than we are—
>   Something that swings the spirit to a star."

On May 25, 1920, under the auspices of the conservation committee of the Twentieth Century Club, six trees were planted in Roosevelt Park in memory of Major Hartwick. A bronze tablet, suitably inscribed, has also been placed near the trees.

It is fitting that the closing words of this all too brief review of Edward E. Hartwick's life should be those of the one who was closest to his heart—his wife. Mrs. Karen B. Hartwick composed the following verses on May 28, 1917, and dedicated them to her husband.

> "*America, come forward, hear the call,*
> *America, thou keeper of the light.*
> *Carry it across the water,*
> *Let not thy spirit falter,*
> *For dark despair clouds many a happy land.*
> *Liberty, thy guardian angel,*
> *Liberty for all, in danger,*
> *America, come forward, sword in hand.*
>
> "*America, we need you, comes the call,*
> *America, our sister, great of heart.*
> *Little Belgium's been assaulted,*
> *Starved and beaten by the vaunted*
> *Knights of Kultur from the ruthless Prussian band.*
> *France, who saved you once, is bleeding,*
> *England mother, too, is pleading,*
> *America, come forward, lend a hand.*
>
> "'*America, come forward, Freedom calls,*
> *America, I need your strength, your might.*
> *Here's task worth any price,*
> *Toil and pain and sacrifice;*
> *Sound the silver bugle thro' your land.*
> *Men enslaved shall be made free,*
> *Liberty enthroned be,*
> *America, God speed you, forward all.*' "

## Chapter III

*Diary of Major Edward E. Hartwick from April until July, 1898, During Time of Voyage to Cuba and First Action There*

APRIL 17, 1898, SUNDAY: Left Leavenworth at 4:30 p. m. Arrived at Grayling on morning of the 19th.

APRIL 22, 1898: Left Grayling for Chickamauga National Park, per telegraphic instructions. Left Cincinnati at 10:00 p. m. Reached Chattanooga about 6:00 a. m. April 23rd, Friday. Reported for duty with regiment to Colonel Hamilton. Regiment went into camp in park in evening. No bedding, so slept in Chattanooga. Captain Hubert got a room with me.

APRIL 24TH, SUNDAY: The 9th moved camp to near Vimard House.

APRIL 30TH: Broke camp and marched to Chattanooga over the Rossville Road. Left Chattanooga for Port Tampa at 4:00 p. m.

MAY 2ND: Arrived at Port Tampa, and went into camp near town at edge of bay south of R. R. Found troops "B" and "F" in camp. Joined by "D" and "I" in afternoon. In camp here until June 8th.

### COMMAND
Troops A, B, C, D, E, F, G, H, I and K

LIEUTENANT-COLONEL HAMILTON
MAJOR FORBUSH
CAPTAIN DIMMICK
CAPTAIN STEDMAN
CAPTAIN FINLEY
CAPTAIN TAYLOR
CAPTAIN MCBLAINE
CAPTAIN POWELL
CAPTAIN WRIGHT

CAPTAIN GUILFOYLE
CAPTAIN GERRARD
LIEUTENANT WOOD, Adjutant
LIEUTENANT GARDNER, Quartermaster
LIEUTENANT STEVENS
LIEUTENANT BARBER
LIEUTENANT KOEHLER
LIEUTENANT RYAN

COMMAND (*Continued*)

Lieutenant Horne
Lieutenant McNamee
Lieutenant White
Lieutenant Batson
Lieutenant Armstrong
Lieutenant Hickock
Lieutenant Walker
Lieutenant Hartwick
Lieutenant Stadter
Lieutenant Parsons
Lieutenant McCormack
Lieutenant Cavenaugh
Lieutenant Pritchard
Doctors Harris and Shaw
Cit. Doctor Danforth

Wednesday, June 8th: Broke camp; went on board S. S. *Miami*, Government Transport. Eight troops comprising 1st and 2nd Squadrons under Major Forbush and Captain Dimmick, Lt.-Col. Hamilton commanding. Officers as follows:

Lieutenant-Colonel Hamilton
Major Forbush
Captain Dimmick
Captain Hughes
Captain Stedman
Captain Finley
Captain Taylor
Captain McBlaine
Captain Powell
First Lieutenant Stevens
First Lieutenant Barber
First Lieutenant McNamee
First Lieutenant Ryan
Second Lieutenant White
Second Lieutenant Batson
Second Lieutenant Walker
Second Lieutenant Hartwick
Second Lieutenant Cavenaugh
Second Lieutenant Stadter
Second Lieutenant McCormack
Doctors Harris and Danforth

Absent:

On Recruiting Service: Captain Garrard, Lieutenants Armstrong and Parsons.

In charge of Troops "I," "F," "L" and "M": Captains Wright and Guilfoyle and Lieutenants Horne, Koehler and Pritchard.

On board transport with 6th Infantry, Lieutenant-Colonel Egbert commanding. 899 enlisted men and officers.

On Friday, June 10th, boats moved into harbor.

Sunday, June 12th, heavy rain. Lightning struck ship.

TROOPSHIPS AND PASSENGERS

1. *Miami*—9th Cavalry and 6th Inf.
2. *Santiago*—9th and 10th Inf. Hdqrs. 1st Div., 3rd Brig. and Hosp.
3. *Gussie*
4. *Cherokee*—1st Batt. of 17th and 12th Inf.
5. *Seneca*—Hdqrs. 1st Brig. and 8th Inf.
6. *Alamo*

7. *Comal*—2 Batt. Artillery 1st—2 Div. Hosp.
8. *Yucatan*
9. *Berkshire*—2 Batt. 2nd Artillery.
10. *Whitney*
11. *Olivette*
12. *Seguranca*—Hdqrs. 5th Corps and Gen. Shafter—1st U. S. Inf.
13. *Omitted*
14. *Concho*—2nd Mass. 13 officers and 306 men—4th Inf. and 25th Inf.
15. *Florida*
16. *City of Washington*—240 Inf.—2 Batt. of 21st Inf.
17. *Alleghany*—Hdqrs. Gen. Wheeler and artillery.
18. *San Marcos*—16th Inf. 1st Batt. 2nd Inf.
19. *D. H. Miller*—7th Inf.
20. *Saratoga*—13th Inf.—1st Batt. 21st Inf.
21. *Leona*—1st Cav.—10th Cavalry. Gen. Young commanding Cav. Brig.
22. *Rio Grande*—6th and 3rd Cavalries.
23. *Vigilancia*—71st N. Y.
24. *Orizaba*—Two Batt. Heavy 4th Artillery, 22 Inf.—One **Batt.** 2nd Mass.
25. *Iroquois*—7th and 17th Inf.
26. *Matteawan*—20th Inf. and two troops 2nd Cavalry.
27. *Arkansas*
28. *Stillwater*
29. *Breakwater*
30. *Morgan*
31. *Knickerbocker*
    *State of Texas*—Hospital Ship
    *Buccaneer*—Hearst's Boat

Strength of Command:  19,575 ⎫ Cavalry and Infantry
                       2,200 ⎭
                         350 Artillery
                         160 Engineers
                       ——————
                      22,285 Aggregate men
                       1,075 Mules
                         683 Horses

## ORDER OF CRUISING

*Vesuvius*  |—1600 yards—|  *Scorpion*

### 1st Division

*Annapolis—800 yards—Castine—Helena—Indiana*

| | | |
|---|---|---|
| 1. *Miami* | 9. *Berkshire* | 17. *Alleghany* |
| 2. *Santiago* | 10. *Whitney* | 18. *San Marcos* |
| (*1600*) 3. *Gussie* | 11. *Olivette* | 19. *D. H. Miller* (*1600*) |
| 4. *Cherokee* | 12. *Seguranca* | 20. *Saratoga* |
| 5. *Seneca* | 25. *Iroquois* | 30. *Morgan* |

*Panther* (left) — *Yosemite* (right)

### 2nd Division

| *Bancroft* | *Manning* | *Hornet* |
|---|---|---|
| 26. *Matteawan* | 28. *Stillwater* | 22. *Rio Grande* |
| 7. *Comal* | 15. *Florida* | 23. *Vigilancia* |
| 8. *Yucatan* | 16. *City of Washington* | 24. *Orizaba* |
| 27. *Arkansas* | 29. *Breakwater* | 21. *Leona* |
| 6. *Alamo* | 14. *Concho* | |

*Wompatuck* (left) — *Eagle* (right)

### INTERNATIONAL SIGNAL T. C. F.

| I. | *Indiana* | H. | *Annapolis* | A. C. | *Eagle* |
| T. | *Detroit* | A. T. | *Panther* | A. W. | *Wasp* |
| A. C. | *Scorpion* | A. H. | *Hornet* | | |
| V. | *Vesuvius* | N. G. | *Manning* | | |
| E. | *Helena* | K. | *Bancroft* | | |
| N. | *Castine* | N. W. | *Wompatuck* | | |

JUNE 13TH: Transport began moving about 9:00 a. m. *Miami* moved at 5:07 p. m. Anchored inside bar near quarantine.

JUNE 14TH: At 3:30 a. m. fleet in order for cruising moved out of harbor and sailed south at quarter speed. Route taken supposed to be to Santiago de Cuba.

JUNE 15, WEDNESDAY: Fleet continued southward. Passed Dry Tortugas at 7:00 p. m. and Rebecca Shoal about 9:30 p. m. Joined at night by *Indiana* and other boats.

JUNE 16, THURSDAY: Morning found fleet moving almost due east. The fair weather continues. Complete convoy given above is with us.

JUNE 17, FRIDAY: Fleet continues south, east and southeast. Weather good—slight showers. At evening sea somewhat rough. At 7:00 a. m. the litter of islands of Cuba seen—first sight of Cuba—the islands north of Cayo Romano. At noon passed Cayo Lobos Lighthouse. At sunset just north of Muertos (suppose that we will be at Inagua Island on Saturday night, tomorrow).

JUNE 18, SATURDAY: Morning found fleet at a dead stop. At 11:00 a. m. again moved southeast, 40 miles made during night—at 3:30 passed Cape Lucrecia—fair weather.

JUNE 19, SUNDAY: At 9:00 a. m. passed Inagua Island—turned south at 11:00—sea growing rough.

JUNE 20TH: Morning found us steaming northward, then northwest, so we concluded we are making for some port. At 10:00 a. m. it seems as if we are going into Guantanamo. All are well so far; 4:30 p. m. have sighted some strange boats. We have not been at Guantanamo, but we are twenty miles south of Santiago harbor and have been lying here till now when we are running southward.

JUNE 21, TUESDAY: 4:00 p. m. Are still opposite the "Morro" about fifteen miles off. Last night we lay farther out, but returned this morning. It has rained today. Saw my first water-spout about two miles off.

WEDNESDAY, 22ND: Daybreak found us steaming eastward nearer to land, about eight miles off. We were formed last night for landing at Daiquiri, a small town about twenty-five miles east of Santiago. At 6:30 we were stopped about a mile from shore—almost the nearest transport. The village was afire. A grand and beautiful picture. The tall mountains carpeted with green and the town in flames, with the column of smoke curling up among the crags. At about 8:00 o'clock the signal was given for "Lawton to put his command in boats." About 8:30 some of the naval boats began firing about four miles from us. We do not know what they are firing at. We have grown weary from waiting to be put ashore. It is 9:45 when suddenly we are startled by a dull roar near us. It is from the men-of-war not 600 yards from our port. And now the five men-of-war are firing. We look toward the heights of the shore not over 2,000 yards off. Puffs of smoke are rising there. It looks as if batteries from the shore which have been hidden among the trees are replying. We wonder why they don't fire on us. Then it occurs to us that the puffs of smoke are from our own shells, bursting and throwing up the rocks. So we feel safer. But have had the sensation of feeling that we are under fire. Now the firing has ceased and we see a line of boats crowded with soldiers being towed towards land by steam launches. Gradually they draw nearer and we finally see them climbing on a wharf. They are shouting and cheering. Part of our corps, the 2nd Division, has landed—our turn will come soon. No, I was mistaken. we have been waiting all day and only about 2,000 men have been landed. We will pass the night on board.

June 23rd: We are still on board. They have begun taking off the 6th Infantry. We may get off today, but there is no telling. Two days ago the ship mess was closed to us, as they have run out of what little stuff they had—and now all of us are running our own mess. A number have been doing so since the first day on board, as that was enough for them. 1:00 p. m., all of the 6th have landed and all of the 9th but "C," "B" and "H" troops. The wind has come up, so they have not been landed. The regimental quartermasters are to remain on board until the cargoes are landed, so I am to stay—as I am acting regimental quartermaster. At 3:00 p. m. we are moving west to a point five miles east of Santiago where we are to land this afternoon. It is one of the places bombarded yesterday. Two or three other transports are to debark there with us.

JUNE 24, FRIDAY: The remaining troops of the 9th were landed last night about 9:00 p. m.—other transports were anchored near us and landed their men this morning. Heavy rain last night. Went ashore this morning to arrange about landing the cargo—could make no arrangements so returned to boat—difficult landing. Siboney is the name of the place. The troops are marching up from Daiquiri, an eleven-mile march. This morning the 1st Regiment of Volunteer Cavalry, dismounted, was sent out to relieve the troops on duty last night. They ran into an ambush about two miles inland toward Santiago—several were wounded—don't know the total damage done—all troops on shore sent to reinforce them. They have been landing horses today—they swim them ashore behind boats—have been sounding stable call to aid, but some horses have been drowned. The navy have been bombarding shore about four miles west from here.

JUNE 25, SATURDAY: Am still aboard *Miami*. The troops "H," "C" and "D," which were landed here and which went to the front, returned last night. Report a hard march—held the front line all day—didn't fire a shot. Captain Capron, 1st Volunteer Cavalry, died and was buried in the village—died of wound received yesterday. It is reported that Captain Knox and Major Bell are severely wounded. Two thousand Cubans brought in today.

SUNDAY, JUNE 26TH: I find that the name of the village here is not Altares, but Siboney. The fight on the 24th was brought on by the 1st Volunteer Cavalry—racing against the rest of the line in order to be first in the fray. Well, they succeeded, but it was a foolhardy move and not military—and not sanctioned by orders. They simply ran into a hornet's nest, without a semblance of proper military formation. Of course, the rest of the line became involved and the 1st and 10th Regular

Cavalry lost a few, killed and wounded. The three troops of the 9th were on shore when word came that the volunteers were being cut up and needed help. Without other order than that of his own discretion, Captain Dimmick rushed the "H," "C" and "D" troops to the assistance of the volunteers. They arrived just in time and were heartily welcomed by the volunteers. They pushed on about 800 yards beyond the line of the volunteers. In their hurry the volunteers had thrown aside all their packs and rations. The 9th passed a few stragglers and skulkers, but the majority of the 1st Regular Cavalry volunteers fought with great reckless bravery. (Their adjutant proved himself a coward.) With proper training the 1st Volunteer Cavalry would make an invincible body, but through bad management they lost unnecessarily. Our line is in sight of Santiago, but it is reported that there will be no further forward movement until the Corps is properly organized.

MONDAY, JUNE 27, 1898: The *Miami* has not yet discharged her cargo—few of the transports have. The engineers are erecting a small wharf to aid in discharging the cargo. We are surrounded by some boats of notoriety —the *City of Washington*, the *Three Friends*, and Clara Barton's hospital ship, *State of Texas*. The Red Cross boat lay alongside of us and gave us some newspapers, the latest two weeks old. It was a goodly sight just to see a few tidy and neat American women. About all of the horses have been landed—a number drowned in swimming. This morning they were landed in the flat-bottomed tug boat *Laura*. The 1st squadron of the 9th gets no more field service at present than do I. They are guarding supplies at Daiquiri, while I am doing the same thing on the boat. My squadron goes out again today. "E" troop joins it from Daiquiri, so it will be complete. I have had one of my boyhood wishes gratified. I remember once expressing the wish that I could have all the bananas I could eat. Well, I have now hanging in the cabin a half-dozen big bunches and have given away many. I don't try the mangoes and coconut, but am yet fond of bananas.

JUNE 28TH: Left the boat at 5:00 p. m. yesterday, taking the men of my squadron, and marched six miles inland to join my regiment. Reached their camp at 7:45 p. m., June 27th. When morning broke I looked out of our "pup tent" and saw Santiago about five miles in our front. Our division is all together with the exception of the 1st Squadron of the 9th Cavalry, which is at Daiquiri guarding supplies. The daily rain came according to schedule and wet us all. After it ceased we had to dry our blankets around the cook fires. Our diet now is hard tack, bacon and coffee—today I found some mangoes. Spanish spy caught—turned over to the Cubans who captured him—they hanged him. We are about two miles from the pickets.

JUNE 29TH: Still in camp. Rain as usual, only harder. Everything wet but blanket and tooth-brush. The two regimental bands in camp played this evening and cheered us all. The men stand around during the rain in their shirts and some in not even a smile. By so doing they keep their clothes dry.

JUNE 30TH: Muster and inspection. Took horse and went to Siboney for several other officers, for clothing, etc. Returned at sundown. Found the road crowded with regiments on the move or stalled waiting for others to move. Found the 9th about 400 yards from what had been our camp, with one man watching my haversack and slicker. They were stalled as others I found. We waited two hours and then finally moved on towards Santiago. After a tedious five hours' night march along slippery, muddy roads, through miasmatic vapors and mountain streams, we were halted. Passed the field hospital. In whispers we asked each other where we were, but none knew. We were near the ruins of some old *hacienda*, which the next day we learned was El Poso.\* The lights of Santiago could be dimly seen and we lay down on our arms at 12:30, wondering what would be our duty for the morrow. I lay down beside someone whom I thought to be a Rough Rider.

JULY 1ST: Awoke before daylight. The stars were still

\*Meaning "The Pit."

winking at me—cold and stiff—the stranger at my side was sitting up and I recognized in the darkness what seemed to me to be Captain Mills of the 1st Regiment Cavalry. I asked, "Is that you, Mills?" and he extended his hand, "Well, Hartwick, is it you?" We chatted of Leavenworth for a moment and then went about our coffee-making. Poor fellow, he was shot through the forehead, but miraculously escaped death. A breakfast at 4:30 of coffee and bacon and hard tack—and a wait of two hours for orders. Suddenly the cannon firing before (El) Caney, about four miles on our right, begins at 6:30 and during which Grimes Battery is going into battery (action) on the hill in front of El Poso about 300 yards from us. All the cavalry was up with us and we got orders to follow the Cubans in advance of the Cavalry Division. Moved out on the road towards Santiago in column of twos along the muddy road. We had advanced about 300 yards when we found the Cubans halted and we were ordered to march on and pass the Cubans—(see report of Captain Dimmick). This order was carried out and Colonel Hamilton was ordered to throw out an advance guard. I was put in command of the advance party by Lieutenant McNamee (my troop commander) with orders to go to the river and halt. I placed two men, Private Prince and Private Cruise as the "point" (Prince was shot later in the day) with Sergeant Jackson in charge of them. I followed the sergeant with the advance party following me in single file with intervals of 30 yards. It was impossible to throw out flankers. When the river was reached we halted and, while waiting, the shelling from El Poso began. We were withdrawn and I was told in forcible language by Lieutenant McNamee not to go so far from the support. I was acting strictly according to orders. He afterwards told me I had done all right, but told me we were going too far and that he had been asked by the Acting Adjutant General if he intended to take Santiago by himself. We were withdrawn and afterwards advanced and crossed the stream. I was the first officer to cross the San Juan River. After going about 300 yards across the river the point was halted and flankers thrown out.

Lieutenant McNamee came up, as did Captain House. General Hawkins and staff followed shortly after as did the advance of the 6th Cavalry. We were then withdrawn about 200 yards and placed as in Captain Dimmick's report. We lay in the grass some time, when the Spanish opened fire, evidently about 700 yards off. It was my first experience of the kind, as it was of all but a few of the older officers. Leaves fell from the trees and dust flew out of stumps. I thought it would be impossible for a man to walk and live in such a fire. The waiting was an awful strain, but yet I dreaded to rise. The men became impatient and wished to move or fire. McNamee called to me, "Where is Captain Dimmick? I want to know who is on our front." I replied that I didn't know. "Shall you go to Captain Dimmick or shall I?" Of course, that was meant for me to go and how I dreaded it, for I thought it would be to get hit. After I had been up a minute and not killed, I felt quite safe. I found Colonel Hamilton, who said, "Mr. Hartwick, Lieutenant Wood has been wounded. I want you to help me in his place." I asked if Wood was seriously hurt and he said he thought not. I was sent by him to different parts of our lines and also helped McNamee to keep "H" troop in line and together, as it was difficult to do owing to the thick undergrowth. We would rush forward about thirty yards and then lie down, excepting the officers who had to keep standing. Shortly after we had reached the foot of the first hill in front of San Juan Hill, Roosevelt's men came up, Roosevelt mounted. He said, "I don't like this. I want to go forward." I replied that we all wanted to go, but were ordered to keep in touch with the 6th Cavalry on our left, but it had moved off to the left flank and the 1st Cavalry had taken its place. Shortly afterwards the command forward was given and I stepped back and called to Colonel Roosevelt that the command had been given, when he took off his hat and we joined in the cheer and charged. Almost immediately, Colonel Hamilton called to me, "Hartwick, take twenty men of 'H' troop and come with me." I got as many men as I could and followed. One man, Private Prince, was shot near me as we went up, and when the top was reached I saw Private Craig holding his left wrist dripping with blood. Shells were bursting and men falling. I took out my handkerchief and bound his (Craig's) wound. We had gone about thirty yards along the crest when the Colonel threw up his hands, turned, staggered back and fell. I grabbed at him, but barely caught him. He was almost instantly killed—shot through the neck while he was facing them. Lieutenant Hays, 1st Volunteer Cavalry, and a 9th Cavalry man helped me carry him about thirty yards below the crest, when I went to report the colonel's death to Captain Dimmick and our brigade commander, Colonel Carroll. I told him I thought Hamilton was going to cover our right flank and he said, "Those were my orders," and started in that direction, where he was wounded a few minutes later. Soon after we were ordered forward to the next line of hills and advanced as the infantry, Kent's Division, was charging on our left. After reaching there, Lieutenant McNamee said the 9th was ordered back. But we decided we would not go back and I went with a request to General Sumner, asking that we could stay on the firing line. We afterwards held the right of the line, reinforced by the 13th Infantry. Here we remained until the morning of the second. No sleep that night and no blankets—only the wet, high grass.

JULY 2ND: Morning came and I was shaky with a chill—the firing opened—two men wounded and a mule killed—moved to the left, relieved by Chaffee's Brigade—joined the 3rd Cavalry near the San Juan house.

### LIST OF CASUALTIES
1st Squadron, 9th U. S. Cavalry, before Santiago de Cuba on July 1st, 1898

Killed:
LIEUTENANT COLONEL HAMILTON
TRUMPETER LEWIS FORT, "H" troop
PRIVATE JAMES JOHNSON, "H" troop
PRIVATE PRINCE, "H" troop (mortally wounded)
Wounded:
CAPTAIN CHARLES W. TAYLOR
FIRST LIEUTENANT W. S. WOOD

Quartermaster Sergeant Thos. B. Craig, "E" troop
Private Hugh Einne, "E" troop
Private Jacob Tull, "E" troop
Private Alfred Wilson, "E" troop
Sergeant H. F. Walls, "D" troop
Private B. H. Bullock, "D" troop
Private William Turner, "D" troop
Corporal John Mason, "H" troop
Private Edward Nelson, "H" troop
Private Edward Davis, "H" troop
Sergeant Adam Moore
Corporal Einne, "C" troop
Private Cuppen, "C" troop
Private Gandy, "C" troop
Private Warren, "C" troop
Private Henry, "C" troop

July 2nd
Assistant Surgeon Danforth killed.

Killed on 1st and 2nd................................... 5
Wounded............................................... 18

After July 1, 1898 until the 23rd, the diary of Lieutenant Hartwick was scribbled in rough notes on an army surgeon's prescription pad. These fragmentary notes, which were intended for later revision and rewriting, convey in few words something of the events in which he participated during those disagreeable days in the trenches before Santiago. This brief, but interesting, record follows:

July 1st*: Night on hill in wet grass. Hard tack among refugees. General Miles arrived and inspected right of line. I did not sleep, but lay and sat most of the time by a small fire of the 13th Infantry, who were on our left. I made some coffee and shared it with Lieutenant Reed. We kept warm by "spooning" each other. Colonel Humphrey and pack train came up with ammunition for Lawton's command, who did not come up until after reaching there. Lieutenant McNamee said we were ordered back, but we decided we would not go back and I was sent back to get permission to stay. General Sumner told me we could remain on the firing line. We afterwards held the right of the line, where we remained

*Record beginning after the day's battle.

till morning. We fought all day and we lay on our arms in the wet grass all night.

JULY 2ND: General Chaffee relieved us with the 12th Infantry. They were afterwards moved and the 1st Cavalry took their place. We were moved this day near the 3rd Cavalry and at sundown the brigade was moved so that we held the trenches on the left of the Rough Riders. Buried Colonel Hamilton. During the night the Spanish attacked the line on our left and the fire was hot from them over our heads for many minutes. We did not reply, but lay awaiting the necessity to do so. That moment didn't come and we slept comparatively well the rest of the night.

JULY 3RD: Desultory firing from the Spanish trenches made it dangerous to show a head out of the trenches. (Rained every day but the 1st up to the 7th.) Truce—ask to surrender or would be bombarded within twenty-four hours. Joined at evening by Leighton.

JULY 4TH: Morning *Cervera* destroyed. Bombardment at night—twice extended (meaning truce).

JULY 5TH: Exodus of refugees. Truce twice extended till 6th. Rain—poison—message read.

JULY 6TH: Bomb proof (shelter) begun. Hobson relieved. (Truce) extended till 10:00 a. m. on 9th, when navy and army are to bombard.

JULY 7TH: No firing. Truce in force. No rain.

JULY 8TH: Went to Siboney for clothes off *Miami*. Couldn't get them. No rain.

JULY 9TH: Offer from Spaniards to surrender town if could move out with arms and proceed to north coast—telegraph to Washington—went with Leighton to (see) Caney refugees. Deserter surrenders.

JULY 10TH: Hard tack, corn. On 3rd message fired on —sent into trenches. At 3:00 p. m. unconditional surrender. At 4:00 p. m. end of armistice. Jefferson and Duncan wounded. Powell killed. Trenches all night. Speech. Paper, *Chicago Record*.

JULY 11TH. Relieved in trenches at daybreak. Spanish speech and calls. Two shots disturbed. Desultory firing till 1:00 p. m. Armistice. Weak bombardment. 1st

Volunteer Cavalry moved to right. Reinforcements that arrived on the 10th moved up to our right. Hardest rain thus far began at night. Most everyone wet.

JULY 12TH: Still raining. Armistice continues. Am damp from so much rain. Many sick among the men, who are nearly all wet. Have a dry spot about three feet long under my piece of canvas. 16th Infantry moving to the right, also four batteries have come up. Have not had my clothes off since the 3rd, nine days ago. Have had one rain bath since June 30th.

JULY 13TH: Armistice still on. Rumor that Linares has offered to surrender on terms that would be satisfactory to Spanish honor. It is said that Shafter has done all that Linares could wish to strengthen Linares' position. Refugees moved out. Have water and beef. Shafter is said to have refused the offer of the navy to lend us guns. No confidence in Shafter. Went with Stevens who put up head-board. Washed my clothes in the rain several times. Have not had a blanket since June 28th. But with my raincoat I keep quite comfortable. We are very anxious to get to our luggage, as my shoe strings and trousers and stockings are all but worn out.

JULY 14TH: Armistice still on. Rain last night. At 10:30 a. m. word received that the Spaniards had surrendered. Miles, Shafter and Wheeler are between the lines fixing terms of capitulation. Leighton is occupying the time digging up tarantulas. He has caught some big ones. Tarantulas and scorpions are plentiful. I have bathed in the rain, and washed my clothes in the rain several times.

JULY 15TH: The commission is still negotiating the terms of surrender. This forenoon Stevens and I rode to the right of the line to the 12th Infantry camp and had a good view of the bay and town. Mr. Acres of the *London News* took breakfast with us. Leighton has gone with him. Terms of capitulation concluded here at 3:00 p. m. today. No rain yesterday or today. Have been a little under the weather today, but hope to be O. K. by morning.

JULY 16TH: Went to Shafter's headquarters about three miles to the rear for mail and also for commissions. Went with Cavenaugh. Poor old horse. Have had no grain. We finally reached there. Got a few potatoes, beans and onions—and two sacks of mail. Shafter just received word that the terms of capitulation were accepted by both governments. Camp moved up on hill top.

JULY 17TH: Order published. Shafter staff and all general officers with provost guard line. Spaniards in two lines. Shafter rode forward to shake hands with Toral. (The order mentioned by Lieutenant Hartwick follows:)

Headquarters 5th Army Corps, Before Santiago de Cuba<br>July 16, 1898

COMMANDING GENERAL,
CAVALRY DIVISION

Sir:—The commanding general directs you to report with your staff to his headquarters at 8:45 a. m. tomorrow, to accompany him to receive the surrender of General Toral. He directs each general officer in your division to report with his staff also. Have your regiments drawn up on the lines from 9:00 to 9:30 a. m. At 11:45 a. m. all troops will again be put in line and at 12:00 o'clock a salute of twenty-one guns will be fired from Captain Capron's battery, which will indicate that the American flag is being hoisted over the governor's palace. Bands will play the Star Spangled Banner and other national hymns and the men will cheer.

Very respectfully,<br>E. G. MCCLERNAND,<br>A. A. G.

The procedure carried out and G. O. (general order) No. 24 read:

Washington, D. C.<br>July 16, 1898

GENERAL SHAFTER:

The President of the United States sends you and your brave army the profound thanks of the American people for the gallant achievement at Santiago, resulting in the surrender of the city and all of the troops under General Toral. Your splendid command has endured not only the hardships and sacrifice incident to campaign and battle, but in stress of heat and weather has triumphed over obstacles which would have overcome men less brave and determined. One and all have displayed the most conspicuous gallantry and earned the

Hartwick Memorial Monument in Woodlawn Cemetery, Detroit

This memorial was designed by W. Liance Cottrell, artist-architect of New York City, and executed by Julius C. Loester, Jr., sculptor, also of New York City

gratitude of the nation. The heart of the people turns with tender sympathy to the sick and wounded. May the Father of Mercy protect and comfort them.

(Signed) WM. McKINLEY

Talked with Major........, commandante of King's Own. Have been this afternoon visiting with Spanish officers. They do not appear to be such a bad lot. Barber (Lieutenant) has interpreted for us. I have a button that a Spanish artillery officer traded for one of mine. I also exchanged money for some Spanish money. First blanket from Stadter.

JULY 18TH: Camp of cavalry division moved by order of Shafter for reasons of health and isolation. But of doubtful good. Hard march of four miles in the intense heat. Have been sick today. Aggravated the hardship of march. Carried my pack. Camp made in rain. After rain we dry out in the hot sun. Ground is wet from high grass. Sand intrenchments.

JULY 19TH: Have been sick all day. No rain. Hope to be better tomorrow.

JULY 20TH: Remained around camp all day—sick, but better. Camp named Camp Hamilton.

JULY 21ST: Went into Santiago on Q. M. business. Street, houses, town, naked children, drainage, pavement. Rode out with Chilty. Promised lighter. Went back with Barnhart and Paddock.

JULY 22ND: Rode into Santiago with Stevens and Barber. Promised wagons and lighter, to get regimental baggage. Failed to get either. Hired row boat and went aboard transport *Miami*. Did some shopping for officers and returned to camp.

JULY 23RD: Rode into town early. Detail came in wagons. At noon got lighter. Unloaded amount of stuff. Got two wagons sent out with Walker. Lunch, supper and lodging, and bath, on board *Iroquois*.

## Chapter IV

*Extracts From Letters Written By Major E. E. Hartwick During 1898*

*From a letter of February 28, 1898:*
   What are my views about the loss of the *Maine?* They are common with everyone's—Spanish treachery. However, the report of the Board of Inquiry ought to clear all doubt, and we must wait for their report. Of course, all preparation is being made for war, because it may be necessary. And for me, I do not see any probability of a peaceful settlement of the Cuban affair. It is more our affair than was our struggle in '76 an affair for French intervention. If honorable and trustworthy men are ever to be believed, then motives of humanity require that the struggle in Cuba be speedily closed. According to the papers, the suffering of those poor Islanders is horrible, but it is not necessary to rely upon the sensational press. Have you read "Cuba in War Time" by Richard Harding Davis? That tells enough. If an individual has a moral obligation to interfere should he see some starving child tortured by an inhuman father, then has this money-getting nation of ours a moral obligation to interfere in the behalf of Cuba? Peaceably if we can, but forcibly if we must. And I yet think it will be done with force. If it comes to that we may and will lose more or less in lives and property. My risk will be as great as the average; and though life is precious and though I have no craving to suffer from fever or wounds, yet I would most gladly and willingly go wherever orders might send me. Gladly, because it would be my duty to go that way. If war does come—it may not—but if it does, I think the brunt of the fighting would fall on the navy. We could gain nothing by invading Spain and we would lose much. And so they could never

think of landing an army on our territory. Other nations could easily do so. We will, however, most surely land troops immediately in Cuba and force Spain to give Cuba independence, and ourselves indemnity for the cost of the war. We might take Cuba for that purpose. It is the only way we will get the island.

Should U. S. troops be sent there, no doubt the regular forces would go first. But I think the war would be of short duration and fear we would lose more from fever than from other causes.

*From letters written from Camp George H. Thomas at Chattanooga:*

We have been here just two weeks and there is, now, no telling how long we shall remain. All is very indefinite. Our army should have been an organized one before the war broke out—then it would be over now. As it is, the volunteers are not yet organized and so our war board seems loath to move us—a handful of regulars—until everything is ready. But sometime we shall go. You have, of course, heard of Ensign Bagley's death. I knew him when he was a cadet at Annapolis. Captain Derst (or Dorst) returned here today—you know his attempt to land was a failure—his second attempt. Though they drove off a Spanish detachment, killing one officer. The first brush for the army.

*From a later letter:*

Well, the 9th is the first regiment of Cavalry to be ordered to Tampa, which I take to mean Cuba. It is a distinction I hope we shall merit. We are ordered to move from camp at 6:00 a. m. We march to town and entrain there. I suppose we shall leave Chattanooga at about 1:00 p. m. tomorrow. Today we (the officers of the 9th) called on our corps commander, General Brooke. Just now our band is giving a concert and I can hear three other bands playing in the distance. You see the different regiments are encamped about a half mile apart, so that the farthest from us is about three miles.

## Soldier and Citizen

*From a letter postmarked "Port Tampa City, June 5, 1898":*

We have not yet gone, though we were informed that Saturday (the preceding day) was the day. However, everything is in readiness for our embarkation. The transports are stocked with rations and the artillery has been loaded, so I think that by Wednesday night we will be steaming out of this harbor for......? I think it will be some point of Cuba, though many here say we are to go to Porto Rico.

This first expedition will be composed almost entirely of regulars—a few volunteer regiments may accompany us. We will go about 25,000 strong. The cavalry goes with two squadrons to a regiment, dismounted. The third squadrons will come later with the horses and they will be made up mostly of the recruits. You see we have been recruiting for over a month. But our recruits are about in the same shape as are ninety percent of the volunteers. They are uniformed, can march and maneuvre fairly well, but they can't "shoot to hit." Of course they can pull a trigger, but that accomplishment doesn't make a soldier. They will learn in time to shoot, but what a vast amount of ammunition they will waste—and what stores of medicine they will consume, most of them—before they are broken in. What an extravagant and wasteful policy the government has been parsimoniously following in regard to our army! Why, it is a fact that here they have been detailing captains of the line away from their companies to "assist" these incompetent political volunteer staff appointees. The "sons of famous sires" draw the pay, wear the uniform and often get in the way, while our officers do the work, get no increase in salary and no thanks. I am not complaining, only stating facts. It is "ours to do, etc.," though "someone has blundered."

*From a letter written "On board Miami transport":*

We are now lying at anchor about a mile from the pier. Our troopship heads the column. I suppose it is because she is the slowest boat. We came out here yesterday; this is our fourth day on board and we are hardly any nearer Cuba than we were a week ago. However, it is better to be here, as the men can take advantage of the chance to swim, and somebody is continually plunging overboard. There are thirty ships in double column and we have three naval vessels—only one that would do much fighting. There are 899 soldiers on the ship, besides the sixty officers and the ship's crew. So you may fancy that we are not any too comfortable. But one doesn't look for luxuries nowadays. I suppose our convoy will join us outside the harbor. Our ship is named the *Miami*. We have the 6th Infantry aboard with us. Tomorrow it will be five years since I graduated. . . . It was quite a stirring scene when we steamed out from the wharves. As each boat left with a regimental band playing, the crowd gave it a rousing cheer. But I have a joke on Barber of the 9th. He stood on the cabin deck waving a handkerchief towards one of the windows of the "Inn" and an answering signal came regularly until we had gone over three-quarters of a mile, when I saw a launch ahead of us and at the bow was Mrs. Barber. I called out to Barber and told him his wife was watching him flirt with another woman. He couldn't understand till I pointed to his wife who had come out to say good-bye.

*From a letter of June 13, 1898, on board S. S. Miami:*
The ships began moving at 9:00 a. m. this morning, but we did not sail till 5:07 p. m. and it is now 6:07 p. m. and the officers are at dinner. We shall form for cruising outside of the harbor. There are thirty-two ships in the convoy, to be guarded by fourteen naval vessels, only three or four of which can do much fighting. But I understand that before we reach Key West, we will have plenty of protection. With intervals and distances the fleet of forty-six ships will form a column over four miles long and about three miles wide. We have on board almost exactly 23,000 men—that is, officers and soldiers; 1,075 mules and 683 horses, besides six batteries of artillery. The next expedition will bring our horses—for seven regiments of cavalry—and remainder of the corps. It may bring more soldiers, that is, the volunteers. You see we have only two regiments of volunteers with us.

It will be an inspiring sight when we take up the formation I mentioned above. I suppose we shall form outside the harbor, either tonight or tomorrow morning early. We are now steaming slowly in the wake of a pilot boat to get out of the harbor. Last night we had another tropical rain. Lightning struck the mast near our cabin, but fortunately did little harm. Another storm is coming up and it is getting too dark to write. Our cabin leaked so last night that only two or three of the bunks escaped a drenching, so that this morning everyone but three or four had to hang out their bed-clothes to dry. I was one of the lucky ones, who was in a dry berth. The unlucky slept in chairs.

*June 15, 1898, on board S. S. Miami:*
We are now about ten miles north of the Dry Tortugas. Have been having fine weather since the rain. It has been just as calm as it could be in a quiet harbor. We have been steaming along at a slow rate—eight knots. In three columns with the naval boats ahead and on our flanks. Our boat is in the lead of our column and so we can have a view of the fleet. But cannot see more than two-thirds of it and some of the two-thirds are only mast high—away behind us it seems as if they are steadily and persistently trying to climb a hill, but can't get up. We are having nothing of excitement to break the monotony of the voyage—unless it be an occasional shark —or a fish. Well, to be truthful, we have been playing cards. For fun?—no—and not for much money. Just enough to make the game interesting.

*June 20, 1898:*
We have been at anchor, or rather not in motion, since late this forenoon and now at 4:30 p. m. we are moving southwest. We have all been surprised and fooled. When I wrote this morning we all thought we were moving toward Guantanamo. But as we drew nearer we found we were off Santiago and here we have been since morning, lying twenty miles south of the entrance of the harbor. I have just come from the bridge, where with a powerful pair of field-glasses I could see masts of the blockading

squadron—Schley's—at the entrance, and then on the hills the fortifications and lighthouse of "El Morro." It is a beautiful sight with the mountains for a background and our own large fleet hovering around. Now we have steamed up and I suppose are making for our landing place. The band is playing right near my ear, so if this is disconnected and illegible, please excuse it. . . . I have kept a few notes of our voyage and shall copy them in this letter.

*Wednesday, June 8th:*
Broke camp at Port Tampa and went on board S. S. *Miami.*

*Thursday, June 9th:*
Lay at pier all day.

*Friday, June 10th:*
Boats moved from pier into harbor.

*Saturday, June 11th:*
At anchor all day in harbor.

*Sunday, June 12th:*
At anchor all day in harbor. Heavy rain and lightning struck ship.

*Monday, June 13th:*
Transports began moving out of inner harbor at 9:00 a. m. *Miami* moved at 5:07 p. m. and anchored at head of fleet inside bar, near quarantine.

*Tuesday, June 14th:*
At 3:30 a. m. fleet moved out of outer harbor in single column, then took up cruising order in three columns. Sailed south at quarter speed. It seems that we are going to Santiago.

*Wednesday, June 15th:*
Fleet continued southward—passed Dry Tortugas at 7:00 p. m. and Rebecca Shoal about 9:30 p. m. passed just west of Sand Key—joined later by *Indiana* and a number of other naval boats.

*Thursday, June 16th:*
Morning finds us moving due east. We turned east about eighty miles north of Havana. Weather has continued fair—complete convoy is with us.

*Friday, June 17th:*
Fleet continues south—east and southeast—weather good—slight showers—sea somewhat rough about noon. At 7:00 a. m. coast islands seen—first sight of Cuba. Supposed to be the islands north of Cayo Romano. At noon passed Cayo Lobos Lighthouse. At sunset we are just north of Muertos.

*Saturday, June 18th:*
Morning finds the fleet not in motion. We do not know why. Went only forty miles during the night. Our protectors were signalling frequently during the night. At 11:00 a. m. moved southeast. At 3:30 p. m. we passed Cape Lucrecia. Weather has continued fair.

*Sunday, June 19th:*
At 9:00 a. m. passed Inagua Island to our port (left). Two gunboats and one transport turned into island for some water. At 11:00 a. m. sea getting rough—at 3:00 p. m. a number are sick. Have escaped it myself. After leaving island turned south.

*Letter of June 21st:*
We didn't land yesterday, but headed for the open sea, where we drifted till this morning at about 9:00, when we steamed back opposite to the "Morro" and about fifteen miles out. We are so anxious to go ashore. Think how long we have been penned and crowded on these boats and now we are here for two days and can't or "they" don't, land us. It has been raining hard today and I saw my first ocean water spout. . . . It is now just past sundown and I have been sitting outside our cabin with the rest, gazing at the beautiful sunset and watching the new moon and the stars grow brighter. It was an impressive picture. Our last night before landing, for we begin debarking before daybreak tomorrow. As I

sat looking at the distant mountains rising out of the water and forming a crescent of blue, then with the other ships of the fleet tossing with us and around us, I thought how much I would like to preserve the picture for you. Santiago is about fifteen miles from us and we land about twenty miles east from there, that is, if the Dons will allow it. Daiquiri is the name of the place at which we hope to effect our landing. With Schley's blockading squadron, we number sixty-two ships—quite a sight.

*Letter of June 23rd:*
Part of the 9th have been landed and the rest of us are to be landed here, about nine miles nearer Santiago than is Daiquiri. . . . Guess I will continue the copy of my notes, as I left off on the 21st.

*Wednesday, June 22nd:*
Daybreak found us steaming eastward, nearer to land than heretofore—we are about eight miles off. Last night we were formed for landing off Daiquiri, a small town about fifteen miles east of Santiago. At 6:30 we stopped and lay to about a mile from shore. We were almost the nearest to land of any transport. A grand and beautiful picture was before us. The tall mountains clad in green, and nestling in the valley a small village near the water's edge and in flames, with the tall columns of smoke curling and rolling up among the crags. The town is deserted. I suppose it was burned by loyal Spaniards to prevent our landing. At about 8:00 the signal is given from the headquarters boat, "Lawton, put your command in boats." The men-of-war have been bombarding the coast as far as I can see to the west from about four miles west of us. We are all getting anxious to begin landing. At 9:45 we were suddenly startled by a dull roar near us. As I look from the porthole I see puffs of smoke on the hillside about 2,000 yards off; and the five men-of-war about 500 yards from our port are belching towards the shore. It seems as if the masked batteries on shore have opened on us, but no, it is only the dust on shore and shells from the men-of-war bursting there. However, I have had the sensation of being under fire, for we surely thought

for a moment that we were being fired on. It was the preliminary bombardment to cover our landing—and Lawton's division is moving in a long line of small boats toward the town. There evidently is no enemy there and they will land safely enough. It is 10:20 and they have reached the land—they are cheering as the stars and stripes are unfurled—I hope our turn will come soon. 6:30 p. m. Only 3,000 men landed today. We will sleep on board tonight.

*Thursday, June 23rd:*
It is about 9:00 a. m. and they have begun to debark us—the 6th Infantry is debarking and we follow. I am to remain on board until our cargo is landed, as I am acting regimental quartermaster and all of the quartermasters are to remain on board. Two days ago the ship's mess was closed, as they had run out of what poor stuff they had, so all of us are messing with our men. A number have done so since our first day on board—one day was enough for them. At noon all have been debarked but three of our troops and on account of the wind the debarkation has ceased. We are to be landed about seven miles west from here.

*Friday, June 24th:*
The remainder of the troops on our boat were landed last night at about 9:00 p. m. So now there are on board the quartermaster of the 6th Infantry, another officer of the 6th and myself. We have a guard of thirty-two men and hope to land the cargo today or tomorrow. Men are being landed all night from boats near us. We are at anchor about 500 yards from shore. It keeps the navy busy landing troops in their small boats. About three boats yet to land troops. It rained in torrents last night and the men on shore have no tents, as the cargoes have not yet been landed. They have the three days' rations they carried on their persons. Our line is now closing around Santiago, and is about five miles from there. I don't believe there will be any fighting, though, for two or three days. On shore, in the little village of Altares, I can see the crowds of soldiers that have been landed—

marching in different directions—and among them are many Cubans. I am better off on ship than on shore, but I will be glad when the stores are landed and I am with the regiment. It is very difficult to write on board. I have little time to describe or picture the shore. The *St. Louis* kept her searchlight going all night to aid the landing, which is made by the steam launches towing a string of three or four boats—about forty men to a boat. All of the 20,000 men will be landed by noon. I don't know where the stores will be landed. I suppose here, as the Spaniards kindly left a train and engine on the railroad track for us. There are several newspaper boats around us. So I suppose you get better accounts than I can write.

*Letter of June 26, 1898:*
We quartermasters are still on board the transports, waiting to discharge the remainder of our cargoes. The three troops of the 9th that were landed here on the night of the twenty-third are encamped on shore about 400 yards from the cabin of this boat. I sent them this morning all their rations and hope soon to send everything ashore and join them. The fight of the twenty-fourth was brought on, so near as can be learned, by the headlong rashness of the 1st Volunteer Cavalry and, as it happened, only cavalry participated in it. All were dismounted. Had they been mounted it would have been what is expected—that is, that cavalry begins the fighting. But I doubt if it was the intention to do more than hold a line of outposts to protect the landing place here, which by the way is called Siboney and not Altares. The regiments that had been performing outpost duty were withdrawn and Wheeler's division sent to relieve them. As I understand, it was only the first brigade, not ours, the 2nd. Well, it seems that Roosevelt's men were overanxious to be the first to get into a fight, for they cast off their blankets and haversacks and made a race ahead of the center and right of the line—which was held by the 1st and 10th regular cavalry. The growth of timber is so thick that they had to follow the trail, so that when they

ran into the ambush they got most severely punished. Their Colonel sent for help and our three troops which had been landed during the night were the ones to relieve them. No one in authority gave Captain Dimmick orders to go to their assistance, but he used his own discretion and reached the fighting line a half-hour earlier than was expected by the volunteers. As the 9th formed line the Spaniards ceased firing, so that our men didn't fire a shot. Had the 1st Volunteer Cavalry advanced in a military manner they would not have suffered any more severely than the 1st and 10th Regulars, who lost a few men killed and three officers and a few men wounded. The 9th remained on duty till night, when they were relieved. The Spaniards have been gradually pushed back with hardly any more fighting until our first line is within sight of Santiago. It will take days to move our artillery there, and so it will be days before we can be in front of the town. Lieutenant Capron, who was a captain of the volunteer cavalry, was buried yesterday, having lived some hours after he was wounded.

*June 27, 1898:*
Have finally received orders that will allow me to join the troops on shore. I leave a guard here and shall go ashore tonight with five men, and start for the front where my squadron is.

*June 29, 1898:*
Still in camp—rain as usual, only harder—never saw it rain in the United States. Everything wet but blanket and toothbrush. The men stand around while it rains, some in a shirt and some in not even that. By so doing they keep their clothes under their bit of canvas dry. It is hard work to get drinking water, and talk of "keeping off the ground"! However, we are all well so far. . . . In the evening the bands play and the men sing. We can put up with the rain so long as it does not come in the night time, when we would get wet, as we have to sleep on the ground.

*June 28, 1898:*
Left the boat at 5:00 p. m. yesterday. Took the five men belonging to my squadron and marched six miles inland to join my troop. Sent the other men (all but one non-commissioned officer and three men) to the other squadron at Daiquiri. Reached our camp at 7:45 p. m., June 27th. My squadron reached there at 5:00 p. m. When I awoke this morning I looked out of the "pup" tent and saw Santiago about five miles in our front. Our division is all together except the 1st Squadron of the 9th and the cavalry squadrons left at Tampa. The 1st Squadron is at Daiquiri guarding supplies. The daily rain came according to schedule and wet us all. After it ceased we had to dry our clothes and blankets around the cook fire. Our diet is regular hard tack, bacon and coffee. Spanish spy caught, turned over to the Cubans and hanged. We are about two miles from the pickets.

*Siboney, Cuba, June 30, 1898:*
I have come in today from the front to get some much needed articles off this boat for several of the officers. I came in on the Major's horse, but will have to walk back as the horse will pack the articles. What have I got? Two tent flies, two pair rubber boots, three shirts, one toothbrush, a pair of shoes, etc. I will have to lead my horse over the trail six miles to our camp—the 2nd Brigade of the 1st Cavalry division. As it rains regularly every afternoon between 1:00 and 4:00, I will have mud most of the way. Our army is now in front of Santiago, all but one brigade. So with 6,000 Cubans under Garcia we have about 26,000 men to throw into the town.

*July 4th, 1898:*
Was in the fight, but am safe and well. Thank God for it. Have no time to write more—we are almost in Santiago.\*

*July 5th. In front of Santiago de Cuba:*
We are now occupying the second line we captured about a mile from the town. The fight was hot all along

\*This letter from Lieutenant Hartwick to his fiancee was written upon two pieces of cardboard torn from a larger piece, wrapped in paper and held with string in place of an envelope.

our line. One squadron of the 9th was in the advance line. I was the first officer to cross the San Juan River. I don't see how I escaped while so many of our men were killed. I caught our Colonel Hamilton as he fell, shot through the head. Thank God that I am alive. We lost over thirty percent of our officers in the 9th engaged and over eleven percent of the men. There may be more fighting, but won't be so serious.

*In trenches before Santiago, July 11, 1898:*
I suppose you have read of the fight of July 1st. Only part of the 9th was engaged in it—eight officers and 160 men. It was my squadron. We were in the front line and suffered in as great proportion as any, though I suppose the 1st Volunteer Cavalry will get all the newspaper credit. They deserve as much credit as anyone, but no more. They reinforced us. We lost four officers and twenty men killed and wounded. I attribute my good fortune to the will of God, for many of our best officers were killed and many men were struck near me. Our Colonel was killed near me—I was acting as his adjutant.

There has been desultory firing since yesterday at 4:00 p. m. Now another armistice is on. We had two men wounded yesterday, and the 2nd Infantry had one officer killed and one wounded. Our men are doing better so far as health is concerned than I would have supposed, for we have to sleep on the ground and take our turn in the damp trenches. I was in last night. The records will show that the 9th fought as hard as any. . . . I don't think there will be so serious fighting as there has been. We are crowding them closer into the town and can starve them out or if necessary carry the place by assault. I hope it won't come to the latter, however. Sir Bryan Leighton is sleeping under my canvas and eating at my fire—he is a bully fellow, if an Englishman. He is a captain in Her Majesty's Cavalry. I won't write you of the pitiful sight when one sees the poor refugees from Santiago. Sir Bryan has just ridden in from a foraging trip. He has brought in some pineapples. Some day I or *we* shall visit him in England.

*In trenches before Santiago de Cuba, July 17, 1898:*
   The formal ceremony of surrender has been gone through today and the Star Spangled Banner is floating over the city. I have been officer of the day. Have been visiting with some Spanish officers just beyond our trenches. They don't appear at all as a bad lot of fellows. I traded a button with an artillery officer for one of his.

*In Santiago, July 23, 1898:*
   This morning I was up at daybreak—breakfast of bacon and coffee. Then a five-mile ride in from our camp in the hills. I am acting regimental quartermaster and came in to get our tentage, cooking utensils, etc. You see we have not had such luxuries since leaving the boat on the twenty-third. I have not even had my blankets. I brought a detail of twenty men in two government wagons. But business is so congested here that, though I had been promised a lighter to be at my service at 8:00 a. m. it was noon before I received it. A tug towed us to our old transport *Miami* and after a few hours of very hard work, overhauling the cargo, we transferred to lighter and to shore about five wagon-loads of cooking utensils, bedding and tentage. I am promised the wagons tomorrow and hope to get the stuff to camp then. In the meantime I am guarding it here. My men sleep on the dock and I have found quarters on board the *Iroquois*, where I had supper, the first decent table I have sat down to since June 11th, the first butter and bread I have seen since June 15th, and I bathed in a real bath-tub. Heretofore, it has been a "wash" in the rain. And think of it, I shall sleep tonight between sheets. Last night my bed was my raincoat and the ground. I hope the war is over. Am thankful for good health. I have been reported for "gallant and conspicuous conduct" on the 1st of July.

*On board S. S. Iroquois, July 27, 1898:*
   I am at present chief quartermaster of the cavalry division and so am in town here, sending out supplies. I sleep on this boat until she steams away, when I shall go on another. I am up at 5:30 every morning. I don't

like the work and I hope I may be relieved soon. This letter was begun this morning, while I was waiting for breakfast. I didn't think I would have time for a letter, so the hurried sentences above. It is noon and past and I have quit work until tomorrow morning. The heat here is terrific. But now that I am getting accustomed to this work, things go more smoothly. You see I have the supply for the six regiments to look after, and everything has to be hauled five miles from here by wagon or pack mule. Today I am engaged in having the mules shod and in giving the pack train repairs and a rest. Eighty-four mules all together. I am doing the work of a staff officer and should be assigned to General Wheeler's staff. Just now, however, I am a line officer, acting for Captain West, who is sick. So long as this boat remains here I shall be all right, for I get good meals here and sleep on board every night. She goes back to the states soon and I will have to hunt for another roost. Have heard that the cavalry division is soon to go back to the states—may it be true! My watch has on its face the photograph of a girl. Do you know whose face it is?

*On board Steamship Rio Grande, August 15, 1898:*
Homeward bound! What a thrill of joy when the propellers finally began to turn and we really experienced the sensation of starting for home—that is, for N. Y. Once in a lifetime. We started yesterday at 1:45 p. m. after a delay of twelve hours, for we were loaded or embarked at 7:00 p. m. on the thirteenth, but owing to overcrowding we waited until morning and then it was decided to leave two troops till later. As the C. O. (commanding officer) of the 9th is junior to the C. O. of the 10th, "A" and "C" troops of the 9th were designated to go ashore and to wait. Imagine if you can the disappointment of those poor fellows. The officers were sick at the order and gave me telegrams to send to their wives, that they could not come till later—all three are married. I might have been one of them to be left had I not been on staff duty—for the juniors were chosen to stay. The C. O. asked me if I wanted to stay. You know my answer.

(The commanding officer referred to was Lieutenant John J. Pershing.)

Well, we left yesterday at 1:45 p. m. It seemed almost too good to be true and Santiago and the Morro never looked so beautiful as they did when I took my last view of them. Now we are resting and enjoying life out of the rain. Actually had turkey on the boat for dinner last night. With the exception of a few hours' very rough weather in going through the Windward Passage, we have had very smooth sailing and we have been out over twenty-four hours. Just passed to our starboard the northernmost of the Crooked Islands. Have not been sick (seasick) since leaving Tampa and I hope the record won't be broken. This boat is a palace compared to the one we came down on. By the way, we sailed on the fourteenth both times. Today we are having music. It was necessary to combine the two bands, as each alone was too weak on account of losses. . . . I am wondering if I will ever get all of my small personal belongings together again. My household stuff at Leavenworth, my horse and trunk at Port Tampa, a trunk at Grayling, and myself and field kit on this boat. . . . It is most difficult writing with the boat rolling so. I trust it will account for so hurried a letter. I have much more to say, but it is trying to write it. Haven't had a glimpse of home land yet. We are now about 150 miles off New Jersey—going north.

# Chapter V

## *The American Cavalry at Santiago*

(Being the manuscript of an address delivered by Major E. E. Hartwick)

I wish at the beginning to correct any impression you may have as to my giving an address. That is the way I notice your program has it, but at the most I can give you only a disconnected talk. This for the reason that addresses are distinctly out of my line and I wish further to add that heretofore I have refrained from even talking of the Santiago campaign. This for the reasons that might occur to any of you should you hear a couple of old hunters or fishermen spinning their yarns. However, when I become older and more garrulous it may be impossible to keep me from talking. In this instance, when I am through you may place the blame on Judge Hammond, as he quite earnestly extended me the invitation, and feeling it an honor as well as perchance a duty, for I believe in these societies, I accepted and hope I may interest you. The subject being the American Cavalry at Santiago, I am excused from relating personal experiences, but shall describe the part taken by our little cavalry force during this campaign as well as my limited vision, together with my knowledge of the official reports, etc., will permit.

I think it not out of place to speak of the unpreparedness in the way of organization of our regular army at the outbreak of the war. This was due to the neglect of the successive national legislatures from 1865 to 1898. Our Congress had seemed to think that owing to our geographical position among the families of nations that there was no use for a regular army other than that of patrolling our western prairies, corralling the Indians; so that after the disbandment of that grand army of 1865 the regular force was gradually reduced and at last organized on the skeleton basis in which the year 1898 found it.

This skeleton formation was such that the army existed in part on paper only. For example, on paper a regiment consisted of twelve troops or companies, but there were actually only ten companies and the strength of these companies was only about fifty percent of what it should be when on a war footing. Consequently, at the beginning, you see, it was necessary to increase the regular force by about sixty percent of what it was prior to the outbreak of the war in April, 1898.

You may imagine the task that confronted our Secretary of War, General R. A. Alger, and I wish to take this opportunity of saying that the country did him a great injustice. He did a great work and deserved reward rather than otherwise, but no official could do the work that should have been done during the previous ten years. Our national Congress was to blame. It takes time to train men and horses. There was neither sufficient supplies nor equipment of any kind, and there was no money available before the sinking of the *Maine* to procure them. Do you wonder that there was endless confusion and needless expense? Little Japan learned wisdom from our folly. I mention all this to explain why our little cavalry force in Cuba was so small, but what there was of it was efficient. Pardon me for saying it, but I say that it constituted one of the best-seasoned, most thoroughly drilled and best-disciplined divisions that the American Army ever possessed.

There were many officers, non-commissioned officers, and privates who had seen continuous service since the Civil War. With but slight exception, all of the cavalry had been west of the Mississippi, and when not actually in the field after the Indians, then on other duty which kept them in the pink of condition.

This was not so universally true of the other arms of the service, though our regular infantry that fought with us was just as efficient and did just as good work.

As you all know, we were mobilized for the expedition

at Port Tampa, Florida. We were organized into a cavalry division under General Joseph Wheeler and attached to Shafter's 5th Army Corps. The division consisted of two brigades under Generals Young and Sumner and the 1st Brigade was composed of the 3rd, 6th and 9th Regiments and the 2nd Brigade of the 1st and 10th and 1st Volunteers, the latter known as the Rough Riders.

Owing to the necessity for drilling recruits and training horses, two troops or companies of each regiment were left at Tampa when we were embarked, so that the fighting strength of the division was not over 2,500 when we sailed.

We were embarked on extemporized troop ships, most of which belonged to the class known as "tramp steamers." The *Miami*, the boat which transported my regiment, had formerly been a cattle ship. A temporary chicken-coop affair was erected out of rough boards, with a leaky, tar-paper roof for a cabin for the officers. The dining tables and sleeping berths were all in this one room, which was to accommodate the officers of two regiments, some sixty in number.

The berths resembled box covers arranged in tiers along the sides of this chicken-coop and one was prevented from falling off his box cover while sleeping or during the rolling of the ship by narrow strips nailed to the sides of the cover.

However, we were much better off than the privates who were packed like sardines in the hold of the ship, and as ventilation was obtained by extemporized funnels made of canvas, their lot was not comfortable, to say the least.

There were about a thousand men on our boat besides the regimental baggage and ammunition, as well as a few horses. I say a few horses, for owing to the lack of transports the cavalry had to go dismounted or not at all. That was another hardship for the cavalry trooper who, as a rule, is attached to his mount, but as all were anxious to go most any sacrifice would gladly have been made rather than be left behind. As it was, two troops or companies out of each regiment were left behind, as previously stated, to take care of the horses and the recruits. Though we were cavalrymen, we were no longer mounted troops, so that when you see a fanciful picture of the dashing mounted charge made by the Rough Riders, please remember that this charge is like other things that did not happen.

There was one mounted troop of the 2nd Regular Cavalry with the expedition, but they were attached to the corps' headquarters and performed the duty of couriers or messengers.

We went on board the transports on the seventh and eighth of June, and on the afternoon of the latter date our transports were underway, but were stopped before we were out of the harbor. This was caused by a rumor of that phantom fleet which caused so much consternation along our coast from Maine to Florida. We were delayed until the 13th of June and the wait was most monotonous, as we were not allowed to leave the transports, but remained idly in the harbor. To our great relief, on the thirteenth, which might have seemed unlucky owing to the number, we again steamed out of the harbor, bound few of us knew where, other than for Cuba or Porto Rico. The voyage was uneventful and took us along the west coast of Florida, to the north and around the east end of Cuba. We were favored with a smooth sea all the way and on the twentieth were opposite the harbor of Santiago. Here we found Sampson's fleet. The twentieth and twenty-first our fleet of transports was maneuvered to the west and south of the harbor, but the morning of the twenty-second found us steaming close in to shore and eastward of the harbor. On that day, under cover of the guns of the fleet, which was blockading the harbor and which shelled the coast at several points, about six thousand troops were landed, this at Daiquiri. By nightfall of the twenty-third, practically all of the men were landed, most of the corps being landed on the twenty-third at Siboney.

The landing was made without resistance on the part of the Spaniards, but was somewhat slow, owing to the lack of lighters and small boats. On account of the rocky and shallow shore, the transports were kept at about a half-mile from shore. There were no docks or piers for the small boats to land at, so that when a boat holding about twenty men was within a couple of hundred feet from the shore it was stopped and the men had to jump in the water and flounder to the shore as best they could. As they were weighted down with blanket roll, haversack with three days' rations, canteen, two hundred rounds of ammunition, and their rifle or carbine, you may understand that the term flounder properly expresses it.

The landing of the animals was a much simpler operation. A trumpeteer who was stationed on shore would sound the stable call, during which the animals were rolled or slid off the gang planks into the water. Nearly all of them, being veterans, mules as well as horses, they would swim towards the sound of the trumpet, but some few had to be grasped by the halters and towed by small boats to the shore. One or two became confused and swam out to sea; others were injured and drowned. This seemed to me at the time a pitiful sight, but one soon became familiar with others much worse. On the whole, considering that we were obeying a rush order and were without proper facilities, the landing was most successful. Two men and some sixty animals were drowned.

Not until the thirtieth were sufficient transportation, ammunition, forage and supplies landed to warrant the corps commander in ordering a forward movement on Santiago. In the meantime, however, a reconnaisance was being made, during which the skirmish known as Las Guasimas was fought. As my regiment was not engaged in this skirmish, but arrived at the scene of the fight when it was practically over, I take the liberty of quoting a description of this fight as given in General Alger's official report. General Wheeler's headquarters were at Siboney on the twenty-third and he was the senior officer there.

That night General Wheeler learned from General Castillo the position and approximate strength of the Spaniards, who were intrenched about three and a half miles west of Siboney, on the main road to Santiago. (These had abandoned Daiquiri on our landing.) He had made, during the day, a personal reconnaisance along the Siboney road, in the direction of Sevilla. General Castillo prepared a map for General Wheeler, giving a full description of the topography of the country, and furnished much information regarding the Spanish troops and their method of fighting. He expressed the belief that, although the Spanish had successfully resisted his attack, they would fall back to Santiago during the night. General Young was present at this conference, and asked permission from General Wheeler to make a reconnaisance in force the next morning. Although General Shafter had given instructions to intrench at Siboney, this was conditional upon meeting no opposition. General Wheeler felt that his orders gave him sufficient latitude, in view of the proximity of the enemy, to determine the position and movements of the Spanish force threatening our advance, and permission was, therefore, given General Young as requested. General Castillo promised to assist with a force of 800 effective Cubans.

Two approaches led from Siboney towards Santiago and the position of the enemy, who were intrenched near where these two roads converge, about four miles northwest of Siboney. The left or westerly trail was scarcely more than a path over a rough and mountainous country, and was known as the ridge trail. The other approach, known as the "valley road," was the main trail to Santiago. When the reconnaisance in force was determined upon, during the night of the twenty-third, General Young directed that Colonel Wood's dismounted volunteer cavalry regiment, consisting of Troops A, B, D, E, F, G, K and L, about 500 strong, should take the ridge trail, while the regular troops A, B, G and K of the 1st Cavalry, 244 men, with Troops A, B, E and I, 220 men, of the 10th (colored) Cavalry, should go with him (Young) along the valley road, together with a battery of four Hotchkiss mountain guns. These two trails were at no place over one and a half miles apart. It was agreed that at about half a mile in advance of the enemy's outposts the two simultaneously approaching cavalry detachments should deploy—Colonel Wood's regiment to be thrown out in the jungle on the right, and join on the left of the line formed by the 1st and 10th Cavalry. The regulars under General Young were to make a feint on the enemy's front, and hold on hard, while Wood's regiment was to make a detour, under a couple of Cuban guides, and attack the Spaniards in flank.

The right column, under General Young, moved out at 5:45 on the morning of the twenty-fourth. After marching little over an hour, the "point," consisting of Captain Mills and two men, discovered the enemy's presence at the place where, they had been informed by General Castillo the night before, the Spaniards would be found. The enemy has chosen his position well. Where Young halted a small creek crossed the road, and an open glade of tall guinea-grass extended for several acres in his front. Immediately in his vicinity, a strong Spanish outpost had been stationed. About 900 yards to the front and right were the principal works of the enemy, on a steep mountain height, where he was intrenched behind rock forts and barricades. On the right ran a high ridge, with a succession of block-houses. The Spanish trenches were 800 or 900 yards in length, and in form of an obtuse angle, the eastern slope facing the regulars, and the southern slope commanding the approach of both the ridge and valley roads.

Realizing that Colonel Wood could not make as good progress as his own column, General Young purposely delayed his attack, in order that the volunteer cavalry might come up abreast of him before he opened fire. However, he at once began operations to develop the enemy's strength. The preparations were cautiously and deliberately made. A Cuban guide was sent by General Young to warn Wood of the nearness of the enemy; canteens were ordered filled from the small creek, the Hotchkiss guns placed in battery about sixty yards beyond the point where the road crosses the creek, and the position of the Spaniards carefully examined. In the meantime, General Wheeler came up and approved the plan of attack and the proposed disposition of the troops.

The attack was to be made by the 1st Cavalry, the 10th to be held in reserve. The 1st Cavalry was deployed in skirmish order in front and to the right of the battery of Hotchkiss guns (B and K on the left, A and G forming the right wing). After a delay of a half-hour the troops began to deploy through the open glade and brush (waiting for Wood). They hardly advanced 200 yards when a strong outpost of the enemy, concealed in an old cemetery between the creek and the road, which ran parallel here, fired a volley almost point-blank into Troops B and K. In this discharge, and in several volleys which quickly followed, while these two troops were seeking shelter, the squadron commander, Major Bell, with K troop at the time, was wounded, as well as Captain Knox, Lieutenant Byram, and Sergeant-Major Ryan. Four privates were killed. The firing from the outposts and intrenchments of the enemy now became very severe, and General Young ordered Captain Beck's troop (A) to the left, and Troops I and B, all of the 10th, to the right of the 1st, the fourth and remaining troop of the 10th being held in support of the Hotchkiss battery.

At only very rare intervals could the enemy be seen, but his firing was both severe and accurate. Nevertheless, the seven troops pushed steadily forward towards the enemy's works, always driving the Spaniards before them. The advance was exceedingly difficult, and made under most trying circumstances. The air was filled with the sharp humming of the Mauser bullets, and the underbrush was so thick that at times the troopers had to cut their way with knives and sabres, occasional wire entanglements adding to the harrassing obstacles in the forward movement. The thickness of the jungle made it impossible to keep any regular line, and the advance and support were soon intermingled. It was practically a troop commander's fight, and even an individual trooper's fight, supervision of the single isolated soldiers being almost impossible on account of the dense undergrowth. Throughout this affair, General Young occupied a most exposed position, in plain view of the enemy's intrenchments. Not a soldier went to the rear to assist the wounded; there were no stragglers; and every man, both white and black, conducted himself with bravery and great self-control. All advanced towards the common objective, and with much difficulty finally forced their way through the dense thicket and over the rocks covering the steep heights on which the Spaniards were, and from which they precipitately fled upon our approach. Troops A, of the 10th, and B, of the 1st, reached the summit somewhat ahead of the others, but were joined by A, of the 1st, and I and B, of the 10th.

In the meantime, the left column, under Colonel Wood, was moving rapidly over the ridge trail, which, as already stated, was hardly more than a bridle-path, with a dense and almost impenetrable jungle pressing closely on its sides. The difficulties of the advance were much increased by the precipitous and rugged character of the ridges over which the trail ran. Knowing that his march would be long and difficult, Wood led his men swiftly over the trail, at such a smart pace, in fact, that fifty or more of them are reported to have fallen out of the column from heat exhaustion. Colonel Wood had been notified that a few hundred yards on the Siboney side of the trail, in advance of the Spanish outposts, he would find a dead guerilla, killed in the action with the Cubans on the previous afternoon. Here Captain Capron's advance, under Sergeant Hamilton Fish, discovered the presence of the enemy, and word was sent back to Wood, who personally moved forward to reconnoitre the Spanish outposts. Satisfying himself of their nearness, he silently deployed five of his eight troops before a shot was fired. Some of these were sent in the jungle of the bushes on the right under Lieutenant-Colonel Roosevelt, and part in the clearing on the left, under Major Brodie. Before this deployment had been entirely completed, the action opened. Wood soon found that the Spanish line was overlapping his own, and he was compelled to place seven of his eight troops on the firing line.

The enemy kept up his firing, mostly by volleys, delivered with the precision of a militia company in a prize drill. The singing and shrieking of the Mauser bullets filled the air, and it was a long time before the regiment could find a target upon which to direct its return fire. Notwithstanding the very trying conditions under which these volunteeers received their baptism of fire, they pushed fearlessly and steadily forward. The thickness of the jungle and the use of smokeless powder made it impossible to discover the enemy. The regiment was untried; it had had less than three weeks' drill before being shipped to Tampa. It is true these dismounted troops had an advantage over other volunteers in that they were armed with Krag-Jorgensen carbines and smokeless powder, and, in fact, with all the best accoutrements furnished the regulars. But Colonel Wood had done wonders with his raw recruits, in organization, equipment, and discipline. It was Wood's spirit and genius that made the regiment what it was. Colonel Wood's high qualities served him in good stead that hot twenty-fourth of June in the Cuban jungle. He was at all times at the front, in the most exposed places, with as little apparent concern as if he were on the streets of Washington. His coolness inspired the admiration of his men, who dubbed him "The Ice-Box."

Wood's two squadrons advanced slowly, forcing the enemy back, and capturing, by a charge across an open glade, an old distillery, from the cover of which the Spanish had been doing much damage to his men, and finally driving the enemy out of his position behind the rocks to his second line of defense on the ridge, but three hundred yards from our line. Soon after, Wood's right extended to the left of the regulars, and both joined in an assault, driving the Spaniards out of their main position behind the rock forts, where they were in large force, and supported by two machine-guns.

The Spaniards were completely routed. They left a large number of their dead upon the field. Our troops occupied the enemy's position, and, had it not been for exhaustion, doubtless would have captured much of the Spanish command. So hasty was the flight of the

Spaniards that the road over which they retreated was strewn with abandoned equipment, and ammunition and articles of clothing were found in profusion scattered in and about the trenches.

As soon as General Lawton, at Siboney, heard the firing, he ordered General Chaffee's brigade, which had in the meantime come up that morning from Daiquiri, to proceed at once to General Young's support, if occasion should make this necessary. Finding that he was more heavily engaged than he had anticipated, General Wheeler, before Chaffee arrived, sent the following note to Lawton:

> "GENERAL LAWTON: General Wheeler directs me to say that he is engaged with a bigger force of the enemy than was anticipated, and directs that any forces that you may have be sent forward on the Sevilla Road as soon as possible.
> "W. D. BEACH,
> *"Captain 3rd Cavalry."*

General Chaffee's brigade, however, did not reach Las Guasimas until after the engagement was over. A half-hour after the fight had terminated, three troops of the 9th Cavalry arrived and were deployed to the front as outposts.

Thus you see the first skirmish was fought and won by our cavalry. This small force of dismounted cavalry drove our enemy, numbering from two to three thousand, from an intrenched position that was supported by machine guns. Out of an attacking force of nine hundred and sixty-four men, our losses were one officer and fifteen men killed and six officers and forty-six men wounded.

As already stated, outposts were thrown out and these were gradually pushed forward till the thirtieth, to within three miles of Santiago. During this time the different regiments of the corps were brought up and bivouacked at supporting intervals along the road—so that we were advanced toward the objective and at the same time covered the line of communications to the base at Daiquiri.

Our shelter while thus bivouacked was the regulation shelter tent, called by the soldiers "pup tents." They were about three feet high, six feet long and wide enough for two men. They served to keep off the hot sun, but were little protection from the tropical rains that fell almost daily after the twenty-eighth. During these regular afternoon showers, many of our men would remove most of their clothing and stand out in the open. Thus they kept their outer clothing dry and many took this opportunity to catch sufficient water in the small tent canvas to wash their one suit of underclothing.

On the afternoon of the thirtieth order was given to break camp and be in marching order at about 4:00 p. m. Owing to the narrowness of the road, which on account of lack of use during the insurrection had grown up with the rank tropical vegetation, it was necessary in most places to advance in single file. This made a tedious and slow march. It was necessary to halt frequently many times to let one subdivision pass another. During one of these waits, some regiment was passing us, but could not be distinguished in the moonlight and our men called out, "What regiment is that?" The answer came, "Roosevelt's Rough Riders," but quickly came the rejoinder, "You mean Wood's Weary Walkers." Notwithstanding that the march was slow and tedious through the mud and fording streams, the men seemed in the best of spirits and laughter and joking was the rule. At about midnight we were halted on an eminence from which we could see the twinkling lights of Santiago. We lay down alongside the roadside, each with his arms, knowing that in the morning we would be called upon to assault the intrenched position of the Spaniards. Daylight came and found us on the hill called El Poso. A hasty breakfast out of our haversacks was had and shortly after a battery was put in position in our immediate front and we were ordered to fall in.

Again I shall take the liberty to read from an official report. This time, however, from the original, a report made to the adjutant-general under orders written by myself as adjutant and over the signature of our surviving commanding officer. Our regimental commander was killed and our squadron commander succeeded to his place.

(Captain Dimmick's report follows here, which is presumably the official report referred to by Major Hartwick.)

Headquarters 2nd Squadron, 9th U. S. Cavalry
Intrenched before Santiago, July 8, 1898

The A. A. G. 1st Cavalry Brigade,
Sir:

I have the honor to submit the following report of the part taken by my squadron of the 9th Cavalry in the fight of July 1st:

Shortly after the cannonading at Caney had begun Dimmick's squadron of the 9th Cavalry under command of Lieutenant-Colonel Hamilton, 9th Cavalry, received orders to move at the head of the Brigade and follow the Cubans. The squadron moved in accordance with this order along the road from El Poso toward Santiago about 300 yards, when Colonel Hamilton received orders to march on and pass the Cubans. This order was carried out and Colonel Hamilton was ordered to throw out an advance guard. "H" troop (Lieutenant McNamee) was the leading troop and took up the advance guard formation. Lieutenant Hartwick, commanding the advance party, received orders to advance to the river (San Juan) and halt. This order was carried out. Shortly after this shelling of the enemy's works by our battery at El Poso began. During this shelling the advance party was withdrawn about 100 yards—by order—and then ordered to again take up the advance and to throw out flankers as soon as the river was crossed.

After crossing the river, Lieutenant Hartwick threw out skirmishers to the right, but could not do so to the left on account of the dense undergrowth.

The point advanced about 200 yards across the river when three rifle shots were received from the enemy.

The advance party halted and Lieutenant McNamee came forward with the support and took command. At the time General Hawkins and staff came up and reconnoitered the enemy's lines from this point. Then a part of the 6th Cavalry came up and the advance guard—"H" troop—was withdrawn about 100 yards and moved to the right of the line.

The 9th Cavalry was on the right of the 6th Cavalry in two skirmish lines, "E" and "C" troops in front and "H" and "D" in rear. Shortly after this we were moved by the right flank and then forward a short distance. While lying in this position the enemy opened fire. At this fire Lieutenant W. S. Wood, adjutant 9th Cavalry, was wounded and also two troopers of troop "D" and one of troop "C." We then moved forward by rushes, but without firing. Owing to the dense undergrowth, "H" and "E" troops overlapped the right troop of the 6th Cavalry. This was soon remedied and "E" troop touched the 6th Cavalry on our left with "H" troop on the right of "E." "C" and "D" troops were moved to the right and somewhat to the rear to cover the open wheat field to our right. In the advance from this position the 6th Cavalry moved slightly to the left and the 9th swung to the right, each taking a different objective, ours being the San Juan house. This made a gap which was filled by one squadron of the 1st Cavalry under Captain Tutherly, who had been notified of the gap by Captain Kerr of the 6th Cavalry. Shortly after, the 1st Cavalry came up and formed on our left. Colonel Roosevelt of the 1st Volunteer Cavalry rode up, followed by some of his men in skirmish order. Colonel Roosevelt said, "I understand the 9th Cavalry is carrying this hill by rushes and I am ordered to reinforce you. Where is your colonel?" Colonel Hamilton was then satisfying himself that the 1st Cavalry had formed on our left. At this point the order "Forward" was given and *repeated to Colonel Roosevelt*. The line, composed of Tutherly's squadron of the 1st Cavalry, Dimmick's squadron of the 9th Cavalry, and Roosevelt's Command of the 1st Volunteer Cavalry, charged with a cheer and took the hill. Owing to the wire fences and dense undergrowth, the charge was one cheering mixed mass of the commands above mentioned. Shortly after this, Colonel Carroll directed Colonel Hamilton to send a detachment of men to protect the right flank. While Colonel Hamilton was leading a detachment for this purpose he was shot and instantly killed. At about this time Captain C. W. Taylor was wounded, as were many of our men.

As soon as the death of Colonel Hamilton was reported to me by Lieutenant Hartwick, who was by his side when he fell, I assumed command and ordered a forward movement of the 9th Cavalry to support the 1st Volunteer Cavalry advancing to the crest beyond. Captain McBlaine, troop "D," and Lieutenant Walker, troop "C," on the right, pushed promptly forward, troop "E," Captain Stedman, troop "H," Lieutenant McNamee, on the left. While this movement was taking place, I was sent to have the 1st Cavalry on our left move forward with us. On returning General Sumner directed me to hold what troops I had at that point till the hills in front had been taken. But "D" and "C" and a detachment of the 10th Cavalry had moved gallantly forward and taken the crest in their front—"H" and part of "E" mixed with the 1st Volunteer Cavalry in taking the crest in their front.

The 9th Cavalry was afterwards assembled and held the right of our line, which was reinforced by the 13th Infantry coming up on our left.

The following named officers took part in the engagement and every one is deserving of the highest praise for his conspicuous conduct:

Lieutenant-Colonel J. M. Hamilton—9th Cavalry—Killed.
First Lieutenant W. S. Wood, adjutant—Wounded.
Captain C. A. Stedman—commanding troop "E."
Captain C. W. Taylor—commanding troop "C"—Wounded.
Captain J. F. McBlaine—commanding troop "D."

First Lieutenant C. W. Stevens—on duty with troop "E."
First Lieutenant M. M. McNamee—commanding troop "H."
First Lieutenant H. A. Barber—on duty with troop "D."
Second Lieutenant K. W. Walker—squadron adjutant and commanding troop "C."
Second Lieutenant E. E. Hartwick—on duty with troop "H" and acting regimental adjutant.

The bearing and conduct of the enlisted men in this fight was all that could be desired and served to maintain the good record of the regiment.

*E. D. Dimmick,*
CAPTAIN 9TH CAVALRY
COMMANDING 2ND SQUADRON

## Official Report of Lieutenant M. M. McNamee

Fort Sill, O. T.
October 20, 1898

TO THE ADJUTANT GENERAL, U. S. A.
WASHINGTON, D. C.
(Through Troop and Regimental Commanders, 9th Cavalry)
Sir:—

Having made only a brief report as commanding officer, Troop "H," 9th Cavalry, principally of casualties, after the battle of San Juan, July 1st, 2nd and 3rd, 1898, and understanding since that reports if any made, of troop commanders, were not appended to regimental and brigade reports; I have the honor to submit a full report of the part taken by Troop "H," 9th Cavalry, in that engagement.

The troop arrived at El Poso about 12:30 o'clock, a. m., July 1st, with the squadron and lay down and slept until daylight. After a hasty breakfast we were soon prepared to march, and waited some time for orders, the men sitting down in column of fours.

About 7:00 o'clock, a. m. the squadron was ordered forward and "H" troop being in lead that day, I was ordered to follow the Cubans. The Cubans had filed by us about one half-hour before we started and had gone down the trail that led into the bottom toward the crossing of the rivers and the heights of San Juan. Having marched about three or four hundred yards down this trail, we were halted on account of these men, who were standing still and who blocked up the road. In a few moments the brigade commander (Colonel Carroll) rode up and we were ordered to precede the Cubans. They gave way for us, falling back in the brush and sides of the road, making an opening through the center of their column, through which we passed.

When our column had passed through, I was ordered by Colonel Carroll and also by our regimental commander, Lieutenant-Colonel Hamilton, to move forward my troop as advance guard, till I reached the river and there to halt and take up a position. I accordingly ordered Second Lieutenant Hartwick to move forward the first platoon as vanguard, with "point" advanced about two hundred yards and to push out flankers wherever openings in the dense brush would permit. I followed with the rest of the troop at a distance of about three hundred yards, keeping up connecting files to the front and rear. I also sent out flankers from my reserve wherever a side path was crossed.

When we started to march, our batteries on the hill in our rear opened fire on the enemy at San Juan and the guns of the enemy replied to this fire, the projectiles from both passing over us, as we passed along the road.

We had advanced about one mile when Lieutenant Hartwick sent word back to me that he had reached the river (Acquadores Ford) and could see the enemy and their works distant about 700 yards. At the same time Colonel Carroll and Captain House rode up and directed me to cross the river and reconnoiter a short distance beyond.

The troop took up the march again, Lieutenant Hartwick crossed the ford and moved with the "point" cautiously up the main road and the trail leading therefrom for about 200 yards, when he received five or six shots from the enemy's small arms, the first that had been fired in this action. He then halted and deployed the men in groups along his front. I crossed over with the reserve, deployed it to the right and moved forward in the brush and high grass, until I reached a point on a line with the advanced party; ordered the men to lie down and not fire without orders. Our line then covered the ford and stream a distance of about 300 yards.

Leaving the First Sergeant with my part of the line, I moved over to the left and sent a patrol from the advanced party along a trail that led down the stream. I then went back to the ford to see if the other troop were coming up and to receive further orders.

I saw General Hawkins, at this time with some of his aides, examining the position of the enemy, from the top of a tree, near the ford. The squadron not appearing, I returned to my troop and waited about half an hour. Lieutenant Wood, our adjutant, then came up from the right and told me the squadron had crossed the stream higher, up to the right, and directed me to move by the right flank and join it.

The day was extremely hot and a heavy fire from the enemy had commenced. Lieutenant Wood was wounded, and thinking the battle about to begin for us, I ordered the men as they moved to the right in single file to pile up their rolls and haversacks and retain only arms and canteens. This was done and I placed Saddler Lockman in charge of the property, telling him to seek cover close by. Subsequently before daylight, July 2nd, I had the rations brought up and later the blanket rolls, with little loss of either. Colonel Hamilton formed the squadron in two lines with intervals of two yards between troopers, and distance of about one hundred yards between the lines. Troop "H" was placed on the left of the second line. In this manner we were moved still farther to the right and then forward about 200 yards, made by rushes. All this time we were under heavy fire which seemed to fly high, however, and was probably directed against troops in our rear and still on the other side of the stream, as few men of our squadron were hurt by it then.

About noon we advanced about 100 yards further and both lines became one, Captains Taylor and McBlaine extending their troops to the right. Troop "H" was now the left center troop with Captain Stedman's troop "E" on my left. Meantime the two troops in front had done considerable firing by volley against the position of the enemy on the first hill and house directly in front, and while we could not see them on account of the trees, the fire from this point was severe. The whole line now continued to fire volleys by troop until about 1:00 o'clock p. m. when the word was given to charge. At this time the 1st Volunteer Cavalry that had been acting as reserve came up from the rear and joined our line and the two organizations charged over the remainder of the bottom across San Juan river and up to the top of the hill. The loss of troop "H" in this charge was: Trumpeter Lewis Ford and Private Johnson killed, and Corporal Mason, Privates Prince, Nelson and Edward Davis wounded.

On the crest of the hill troop "H," like others, was intermingled with other troops, but all lined up and poured a rapid fire on the main works of the enemy on the ridge beyond.

At this time the Brigade Commander, Colonel Carroll, was wounded and Colonel Hamilton killed, Captain Dimmick, 9th Cavalry, succeeding to command the regiment.

I rallied the troop, getting some thirty men together at the time, and moved forward, with the general advance on the main position. There being no brush or wire in our front now to contend with, I determined to advance in good order. The other troops in the squadron had been called to the right. I ordered Lieutenant Hartwick to follow in rear; I deployed the troop in line and, placing myself in front of the center trooper, passed over the hill, down the slope and forded the upper end of the lake and moved quickly up the slope to the Spanish works, but the enemy had given way.

Colonel Wood, 1st Volunteer Cavalry, who had succeeded to the command of our brigade, came up and ordered me to move over to the right with my troop and hold certain hills which he pointed out, at all hazards, until I was relieved.

I accordingly moved over and occupied the ground indicated. I sent Lieutenant Hartwick to patrol still further to the right, where he found "C" and "D" troops of our squadron in position. Later the squadron was assembled on the ground occupied by my troop and remained there until relieved, about 7:00 p. m., by the 13th Infantry.

The next morning, July 2nd, the troop moved with the squadron to the left and joined the Cavalry Division, near the center of the line. Here the troop continued digging and occupying entrenchments until the surrender of the Spanish Army and city of Santiago.

It will be seen from the foregoing account that my troop was the first organization to penetrate and reconnoiter the ground to the front the morning of July 1st, and crossed the first river, the Acquadores near its junction with the San Juan, several hundred yards in advance of other troops. The country is covered with dense undergrowth and great caution had to be exercised to avoid being ambushed by the enemy. In this connection much credit is due Second Lieutenant Hartwick, 9th Cavalry, who conducted the movements of the "point" and "flankers" in the advance. Lieutenant Hartwick pushed steadily forward until he was fired on by the enemy and directed by me to halt. This officer displayed great coolness in a very trying and dangerous position.

During the assault and throughout the entire day, by his courage and prompt action, I was enabled to get the best results from the troop. I recommend him for consideration.

As to the enlisted men of the troop, they all did well and displayed patience, courage and discipline of a high order.

I wish to particularly mention Sergeant Elisha Jackson, now Second Lieutenant, 10th U. S. Volunteers, who, during the movements on the morning of July 1st, was in the extreme advance (the "point") and who "during the whole day was ever in the front," and by his example encouraged all about him, also Privates Bates and Pumphrey, who, while the troop was under heavy fire, stood up and moved out from cover the better to see and fire on one of the enemy, who from a tree in front was firing on us, also of Sergeant John Mason and Private Nelson, who were wounded while charging up the hill, near the head of their troop, and Private Edward Davis, who, although suffering from a scalp wound, the blood streaming down his face, only waited to have his head bandaged, when the first hill was taken, and then joined the troop in the next advance.

I feel that the record of the troop would be incomplete were this report not made, and respectfully request that it be appended to the regimental report, now on file in the Adjutant General's office.

Very respectfully,
Your obedient servant,
(Signed) *M. M. McNamee*
1st LIEUTENANT, 9TH CAVALRY,
Commanding Troop "H" while in Cuba.

CHAPTER VI

*Journal of Major Hartwick During His Service in 1917-18*

On Board *U. S. S. Madawaska*
Nov. 12, 1917

MY DEAREST GIRL AND BOYS:

It will be impossible for me to write you in long hand if I am to send you any news, as I would like to do, so I am dictating a sort of daily dairy, as it may interest you.

I know it has been harder for Mother than it has been for me, because I have been busy almost every minute since leaving you, but it is a comfort to know that Nelson has promised to take my place until I get back and that both he and Robert told me that every morning they would make a resolution to do nothing that would not give pleasure to Mother, and also that they will remember that each is the best friend, outside of his Mother, that the other has.

After we left camp we marched to the train and moved by rail to the port of embarkation,* of which you already know the name. The officers rode in day coaches the same as the men, and we reached the port of embarkation in the morning, going to the transport about 7:00 o'clock, after a long delay, necessary for the reason that each man was tagged around his neck with a tag showing his troop number, berth number and meal ticket, which is punched at every meal.

At noon Monday, the day we went aboard the transport, I was invited to have lunch with the captain of the boat, a regular naval officer, Captain Watson. Would rather not have accepted owing to my personal appearance, not having used a razor for forty-eight hours, and was much chagrined to find at the table Admiral Chester, his daughter-in-law, and General Appleton, a National Guard General of New York State.

*The port of embarkation was New York City.

This is the first trip of this troop transport, which is now christened *U. S. S. Madawaska*, formerly *König Wilhelm II* of the Hamburg-American Line, and it seems rather ironical to note the initials of the Hamburg-American Line on the dishes and table service, etc. The boat has been renovated and altered for a troop ship by the navy and is a naval transport, not under control of the army. Captain Watson graduated from the Naval Academy the year after I graduated from West Point. The executive officer is Mr. McCauley, another naval graduate, of the year 1908. There is also an ensign on board who is a graduate, but all the other officers are naval reserve officers, among them being a son of Charles Schwab, the steel magnate, and a son of Mr. Armour, the packer.

The accommodations on this transport were a surprise to me, as I had in memory the transports used during the Spanish War, and I was delightfully surprised on finding my quarters to have a very large bathroom, with running water, both hot and cold, and a fair sized bedroom with regular beds. My room mate is Colonel Bridges, a regular officer, who graduated from the academy four years after I did. We left the dock on Monday, November 12th, at about 7:00 p. m.

*Tuesday, November 13th:*
Sun rose at 6:34 a. m. We found ourselves under convoy of the cruiser *San Diego*, with two destroyers, two other transports, the *Powhatan* and the *Pocahontas*. The armament of our transport consists of two six-inch guns, two three-pounders, two rapid-fire guns and two machine guns. Most of the afternoon was spent in posting our guard of sentinels in accordance with the naval orders, which required about 116 men of three reliefs, being two hours on post and four hours off post. The sea was very calm and the day pleasant. In addition to the regular guard detail of sentinels, we were required to furnish a detail for the crow's nest, fore and aft, and for lookouts around the side of the ship. We had two "abandon ship" drills. Lights were extinguished at sunset.

*Wednesday, November 14th:*
Sunrise 6:46 a. m. This day was marked by a very sad, but impressive event, the funeral of Bugler Davis, Company "C," whose mother is Mrs. Carrie S. Davis, No. 1747 West Ontario St., Philadelphia, Pa., and who died of spinal meningitis during the forenoon. The captain of the ship ordered that he be buried at sea, and the ceremony took place at 3:45 p. m.; the engines in all of the ships in the fleet and convoy being stopped at that time, when the flag was lowered to half-mast, the body, draped in the American flag, brought up on the after-deck, all of the crew and soldiers ordered to abandon ship stations, funeral services read by Colonel White of the cavalry, taps blown by Bugler Petersen, also of "C" Company, and the body committed to the deep at 4:00 p. m. in latitude 40 degrees, 41 minutes, 15 seconds north, longitude 64 degrees, 40 minutes, 30 seconds west. At the lowering of the body, the firing squad fired three volleys, the flag was raised and the fleet moved forward again. One other case of the same dread disease developed during this day. Captain Cutting came on board a very sick man and has been delirious most of the time. The doctors made a test today by inserting a tube in his spine and decided that he also had a mild form of the same disease. I am sure he knew he was sick at the time we left camp, but was afraid that if he stayed behind he might have been regarded as a slacker. We are also greatly troubled with measles, which we inherited at Camp American University, and they had to establish a contagious ward in order to accommodate them. The sea has been calm again today and it seems more like being on the Detroit River, so far as the weather being rough is concerned, than being on the briny deep.

Last night a little incident occurred which pleased the army. We have had very strict regulations not to permit any smoking, lighting of matches or flashing of lights after sunset, and one of the navy petty officers, desiring to fix a boat on deck, asked one of our sentinels if he would permit him to use his blue flashlight, but our sentinel promptly answered that if he did he would shoot him; and when the man was taken to the executive officer of the ship, he was told that the sentinel should have shot him, as he deserved to be shot for not knowing his duty any better.

While we were embarking and the men were marching through the ferry, the marching was suddenly stopped and on inquiry I found that the stop was the result of a soldier refusing to go farther; he had just arrived within sight of the water. He said he did not enlist to go on a boat. However, he proceeded and we had to put him and another prisoner in the ship's prison. All of these prisoners have, however, been released on account of the danger of leaving them locked in their prisons, should some emergency arise which would cause us to leave the ship.

We discovered a private in our command who holds papers as a sailing master, and who has owned his own ship. This illustrates the fact that we have a very unusual body of men. We also found a minister today, when searching for a prayer-book for the funeral services. My orderly today is a graduate of the University of Wisconsin. The sea has been calm again today.

*Thursday, November 15th:*
No event today to report other than the usual abandon ship drill and the fact that after I had finished my dinner I was invited to take dinner with the captain, which invitation I did not feel I could refuse, so in order not to disappoint the captain, I had two dinners today. The sea has been calm and we are still having beautiful weather.

*Friday, November 16th:*
Sun rose at 6:37 a. m. Cloudy. At 9:00 a. m. a storm gathered and the sea has been very rough; orders have been issued to keep the men above deck so as to prevent as many as possible from being sick. Evidently Friday is an unlucky day.

*Saturday, November 17th:*
Lights were turned on this morning at 3:20 a. m. for a

short time, owing to the fact that the storm of yesterday, which continued through the night, broke open an outside door on one of the decks and let in a large volume of water, which flooded most of the officers' state-rooms and caused a lot of discomfort among the men as well. When I awoke, I heard my room-mate using very emphatic language, and saw him in the pale blue light, which is the only light we use after sunset, standing on his heels in the water, with his pajamas turned up to his knees, trying to save some of his personal belongings, which were floating around the room. He, however, soon jumped back into bed and we waited until a detachment of the crew came with mops and buckets and baled out our room. The sea has been very heavy all day and much damage has been done to the furniture, dishware, etc., and I have discovered that when the water got into my room, it wet everything in the bottom of my trunk, so I have had to play laundress and have a clothes line in the bathroom full of my clothes, trying to get the wet ones in shape to put back into my trunk. . . . Sea continued very rough all day. One of our transports turned back the second day out and as the other is only an eleven and one-half knot boat, and we are a fifteen-knot boat, we have to wait for her to keep up with us. We had the pleasure of issuing to the men some nine boxes of tobacoo, which was furnished us on board by An Army Girl's Transport Tobacco Fund.

*Sunday, November 18th:*
Everyone was cheered this morning by finding the sea smoother, although the weather is cold. At the abandon ship drill today the men were put in the boats in the positions they will occupy, and some of the men were taught how to use the oars and obey the commands that will be given them. They are under the orders of the naval officers in this work. Today is Sunday and a very pleasant day for all of us, but since we have no chaplain on board I would not have been reminded of the fact had I not seen a soldier reading his prayer-book. As I am writing there is a concert under way, but it is

hardly a sacred concert. Gave orders today that for the next three days all companies alternating in turn would see that their men were given baths, as after that time we will not be permitted to remove our clothes until we get off the boat, but will have to wear our life belts and the officers their side arms. Found time today to enjoy a salt water bath heated by steam. It seemed quite a luxury and I could almost imagine I was home. All hands were called on deck to witness target practice, but same was suspended on account of some strange vessels in the offing, and do not know whether we will get to practice today or not. Captain Cutting is no better, although he is holding his own. Another case of spinal meningitis has been discovered, making four that have appeared since we left the dock. All of the men are summoned on deck once a day to have their throats examined by the surgeons and their shirts thrown open, the same being for inspection for measles. This, with compulsory baths, abandon ship drills, mess calls, and lights out at 4:00 o'clock well fill in the day. You will be interested to know that we found on board for the 20th Engineers sixteen hundred sets of knitted garments secured from the Red Cross by Mrs. Black, wife of the chief of engineers. These are being issued today and I have written her in behalf of the regiment, thanking her for her thoughtfulness. . . . We were disappointed. Instead of receiving 1,600 complete sets of knitted garments, we found 859 sweaters, 1,530 mufflers, 1,464 pairs of socks and 1,491 pairs of wristlets. Have so notified Mrs. Black.

Because the above is not written in long hand, don't think I have not been thinking of you and the boys. But you have no idea how rough it has been. I never saw rougher weather even when we came over on the *Lahn*. Yet, I never felt better. Not a qualm of seasickness.

*Monday, November 19th:*
This is the morning of the seventh day; accordingly, it should be a day of rest, but with such a restless ocean there is not very much quiet on this ship. True, a great

many of our men prefer to remain quiet so that it has become necessary to have a commissioned officer from each company make an hourly inspection to keep the men above deck. It is a day like the roughest day when we came over on the *Lahn*. There have been no drills today and nothing to break the monotony except mess calls, which come at very uneven intervals—breakfast at 7:30 a. m., lunch at 11:00 a. m., dinner at 4:00 p. m., so that it is a long time from the evening meal to breakfast.

The ship's officers have several times complimented me on the good order maintained by our men, as well as on the cheerful spirit they possess, and on the night that the flood broke through the door and flooded the officers' quarters and decks below, there was very little excitement and what there was, was caused by a reserve petty officer of the navy, who himself got stampeded and reported to the officer of the deck that the ship was sinking and cried out among several of the state-rooms to abandon the ship.

I have several times been wondering how you and the boys have been passing the time since I left, a little over a week ago, and hope that both of the boys have been bringing home hundred marks from school.

Captain Cutting is still in a precarious condition, and if we shall have to abandon ship, the severe exposure will certainly finish him. We have a sick report of fifty-four out of an aggregate strength of fifty officers and 1,543 men; this is about three percent. About ninety percent is measles, so I suppose we will be put in a quarantine camp when we are finally landed.

Today I appointed an entertainment committee with Captain Boetzkes as chairman, for the principal purpose of providing amusement for the enlisted men after we have landed. Understand that temptations are rather numerous to beguile the men from camp, and unless we may entertain them in camp, it will be hard to keep them from getting into trouble.

This letter will not pass the censor, so I am going to send it, if possible, by some friend whom I may find on his way back. If I were not sure that there will be no damage done by it would not write of some things, but it would be pretty dry reading (possibly it is anyway?) if I just said every morning, "I am well."

*Tuesday, November 20th:*
Weather clear, but sea continues very rough; yesterday the entertainment committee took a census of the musical members of the different companies, instrumental and vocal, and the officers were entertained at the evening meal by a vocal quartette from "C" Company. An especially fine singer was discovered, as well as a splendid pianist. Tonight the enlisted men from another company will entertain us, and so on. I find that the men have managed to bring with them various kinds of musical instruments. It was certainly a peculiar concert to see the assembly of officers, hardly distinguishable after dinner, in the faint blue light, somewhat obscured by clouds of tobacco smoke, but all eagerly listening, enjoying the music, some of the songs having been extemporized; a copy of one is enclosed herewith, which was composed for the occasion by one of my orderlies, Wagoner Kraft, the final rendition being the Star Spangled Banner, and it was surprising how many of the officers could sing it. The blue light, which is turned on after sunset, is such that its direct rays cannot be seen at a distance exceeding 600 yards. The port holes are painted black, the shutters are drawn, key holes on the upper decks are stuffed, so that all that can be seen of the ship at night and that at a short distance only, is a very black hulk, looming up over the water line. The trip is getting somewhat monotonous and the only way to vary it seems to be in reading and by friendly groups at cards, among the officers' staterooms. Everyone seems to have exhausted his stock of yarns, so we will certainly all be glad to get on shore. This aside from the misery caused to some by the rough weather. After the white lights are turned off it is impossible to read or play cards, and I find that several choirs are being organized about the ship.

This is our ninth day on board and eight full days tonight since we sailed. Had breakfast this morning with Captain Watson, ship commander. It tasted good—bananas and "cream," shirred eggs, bacon, coffee, toast and jam. The coffee was "Washington Coffee," dissolved in a cup of hot milk. It was contained in a jar about the size of McLaren's cheese and was fine—a half teaspoonful for a cup.

At about noon today the sea began to compose itself and immediately there was more cheer on board. We have been expecting to meet some supply ships—tankers and food—but on account of storm missed them last night. Since the sun came out and a reckoning taken, at 2:20 we turned southward, then westward in a big circle, as if we were heading for home. Someone said he left his suit case on the dock. But we are looking for the tank ship. It seems they did not dare to radio.

*Wednesday, November 21st:*

The sea is quite smooth again, so everyone is feeling fine. We have hardly been moving since yesterday afternoon, hunting the *Arethusa*—name of the tanker that furnishes oil to the destroyers. They remind me of little pigs, each alongside taking milk from the sow through a hose. Well, this maneuver will lose us about one day's time. It is now 1:00 p. m. and we are still stopped.

You did not know it, but I made reservations last night at a theater and took you all to an opera. I awoke about 4:00 a. m. and was disappointed to find I had been dreaming—and I paid just as much for Robert's ticket as for the rest. I have no idea where we are. Tonight it will be nine days out. We must be within a day of the "danger zone," so by four days more we should be landed.

The executive officer is Mr. Cleveland McCauley, a senior lieutenant, and most courteous. I am writing this in his cabin. We have been interchanging "blue light" visits the last four evenings. He has had some remarkable experiences afloat—graduated only nine years ago. He is directly responsible for Uncle Sam having two of Kaiser Bill's boats, worth about a million apiece, both of which King George's navy expected to catch. Last night he gave me two souvenirs of this boat left by the Germans. One is a silver ash tray and the other a *König Wilhelm II* hat band. Mr. McCauley had charge of our navy secret service intelligence department in Mexico, protecting the Tampico oil field, and was directly responsible for ridding that part of Mexico of the Huns. He says that he never saw but one harder "blow" than we have had on this ship and that was in a typhoon on the China sea, when he was lashed to the bridge of a destroyer for seventy-two hours.

We are now in a comparatively calm sea—bobbing about like corks are the little destroyers taking their oil—but this boat has only a gentle roll. We are still "lying to."

*Thursday, November 22nd:*
This has been a beautiful day. Just like being on one of our Great Lakes on a calm day in August—hardly any motion of the sea perceptible. Aside from drills, meals and officers' conferences, I have walked on the hurricane deck, and studied French as I walked.

One of our destroyers has had trouble with her steering apparatus and is being towed by the cruiser. We certainly hope that they may have everything fixed before we encounter any strange ships, as when we do one destroyer hastens away towards the stranger, to make sure if it be friend or foe, and we don't care to be left with a crippled destroyer and only the cruiser to protect us. This forenoon we encountered a large school of porpoises and they came closer than any I ever saw before. You would not think it possible, but the other night one of our captains (2nd Battalion) lighted a pipe on deck after dark. This report has not come to me officially. However, I have given written orders to the guard to have pieces loaded and not to hesitate to fire at any lighted cigar, pipe, cigarette or flashing match. It is surprising how quickly the news of this order has spread. Shall also interview the captain who was so thoughtless and would court martial him if I had received the report in an official manner.

Was just given a confidential piece of news, viz.: that we would be in the danger zone in about 24 hours. That means, I hope, that if we get through all safely, that we will arrive at our port about Monday next—the twenty-sixth, three days before Thanksgiving. It is just fifteen minutes before mess call for dinner at 4:00 p. m. and only an hour more of daylight, when we will have to sit in the pale blue light. The captain has again invited me to dine with him, so, my girl and kiddies, good night.

*Friday, November 23rd:*

This morning dawned most beautiful, although according to the ship's time Old Sol was late, for it was past the hour of 7:00 when he peeped over the watery edge of the world. I was up and on the hurricane deck to see how long it would take him after he started to get completely out of the water. It was just three and a half minutes and the same time for him to get under last night after he took the first dip. About fifteen minutes before sunrise two new destroyers were sighted coming our way and within a half-hour there were in all six new destroyers, so that now we have an escort of eight destroyers in addition to the battleship. I heard one officer remark as he looked at the new arrivals, that "Old Glory" certainly was a beautiful sight, and I thought that it appeared so because of the comfort it added to our sense of security and protection, as much as the appearance of the flag itself. Our visitors are all camouflaged and must be hard to see from the water line, as they are painted to resemble low-lying clouds and water line joining.

Today we were honored by the visit of a couple of whales. Our lookout cried out, "What is that off the starboard quarter of the cruiser?" I suppose that when he first glimpsed it, he was not sure if it might not be a "sub." You see, we have in all fifty-six men from the army and several officers serving in the tops and around the decks of the ship as lookouts, and there is quite a spirit of rivalry between them and the navy as to who can "see it first." The way we are now guarded it seems to me that a sub will be taking grave chances if she tackles us in the day time, and even at night she will be in serious danger and it will be a "scratch" if she tries it and gets safely away. We are all out on deck, as would be the case in August on the Detroit River. It hardly seems possible that it is so late in the year as November 23rd.

We have just changed time to Greenwich time, moving the clock ahead one hour and thirty-one minutes, so there will be no more change of time. The order has come for everyone to wear life belts and keep on his clothes at all times, which means that we are in the "danger zone."

*Saturday Afternoon, November 24th:*
Everyone on decks by order this morning before 6:00 a. m., so that at what is considered the most dangerous hour there would be no one below decks to be blown up by a "sub" and so we could more quickly take advantage of such an emergency. Last night was the first night that we have been required to sleep in our shoes. Yet all are feeling happy and cheerful, though it was quite a wait on deck from 5:30 to daylight. At first so dark that one could not distinguish objects on the ship, but slowly the darkness changed to semi-darkness, then a gray light, then the glow of dawn over the water, when we could begin to count our little destroyers, each in his proper place. We are now passing through a locality where the Germans have sunk most of their prey, so Mr. McCauley just told me, and our captain said he was turned off his bed last night by a signal from the flagship "Submarine— look out for torpedoes on port bow," but immediately it was seen to be a school of porpoises. The officers are making up a pool as to what time "Land Ho" will be first correctly called. It is now the twenty-fourth and the guesses run at various hours from the twenty-fifth to the twenty-seventh. This evening (twenty-fourth) will end our twelfth full day of twenty-four hours each. Have not written any other letters—except official—but will write you a note to go by the regular way—censor. It will probably reach you ten days before this, depending upon whom I find that I know to carry this back for me.

*Sunday Afternoon, November 25th:*
 Well, this is to be the last chapter of this boat-ride diary letter. We are to be docked at daylight tomorrow. I understand that we are in the Bay of Biscay and that we will land at St. Nazaire, the port of Nance, so if this be true it confirms my guess that we will be located on the River Loire near Nevers or St. Etienne. Now that we are approaching land we have lost the mild, warm weather and are fanned by a cold breeze, which I presume indicates that on shore it is wintry weather. We have also lost our smooth sea and the ship is rolling very unsteadily. I am thankful that we have so far passed safely the "sub" peril, yet we have a dangerous gauntlet to run before morning. Twelve hours more should put us out of danger. Have just dictated a letter to the captain and executive officer as coming from all of our officers, thanking them for their efforts in our behalf. I submitted it at conference to our officers today and all were pleased that I had thought of it. It has pleased the captain of the ship and they certainly deserve our gratitude, for they have gone out of their official way and duties to make everything harmonious, pleasant and safe for us.

*Monday, November 26th:*
 Land sighted at 6:35 a. m. Sea smooth and weather clear. We were met by three yachts flying the American flag, all mounting guns forward and aft. Also two French biplanes came out and hovered over us, having the tricolor and stripes on the lower plane and on the tail also. At each end of the lower plane a tri-colored target circle, and we could see mounted forward a large machine-gun, pointed downward. Also a dirigible balloon was flying over the harbor. Our fleet formation was changed to column formation, our escort of destroyers falling in behind us, and we were piloted in by one yacht, the other two sailing along on our starboard.
 I learned that one of our naval lieutenants, a Mr. Huntington, is father-in-law of Vincent Astor, and that Vincent Astor is aboard one of the yachts off to our right

as an ensign in the navy, but not in command of the yacht. We anchored in bay for some hours opposite a town and were finally passed through the locks and are now in the canal alongside the River Loire. We received a great ovation from people lined up on the streets running alongside both sides of the locks and the many apple women in the crowd soon sold out their supplies, which were thrown to us by civilians and our own soldiers who are here ahead of us.

We have received on board staff officers who are giving us instructions, but we are to pass the night at least on this boat, so that the morning of the twenty-seventh will still find us aboard.

The captain of the ship took dinner with us in our mess room this evening, and a few of the army officers, including myself, were seated at the navy table, and the captain handed me a letter complimentary to the good order and behavior and cleanliness of our men during the trip, which order it will give me great pleasure to read to the men at the proper time.

If we are moved into a quarantine camp or other encampment here, we will entrain at once and be sent to our field of operation. It was a very stirring sight to see so many transports in the harbor here, which gives evidence of the immense amount of freight that has been delivered and the gigantic job that the United States has undertaken.

We received the first news of the war since the fifteenth, and it was very good news, as we found that the Italians were still holding the enemy, and that the British had gained quite a victory on the West Front. We are all feeling very thankful. Captain Cutting still continues to improve. He will be moved from the ship to the base hospital.

*Tuesday, November 26th:*
We are still on board the *Madawaska* and it seemed good to get in bed and not have my shoes on, but back to the old pajamas. Our sick are to leave the ship for the hospital in a little while and I hope that we will then

be put on shore. I think it will be in a cantonment for quarantine. I am going to try to get permission to cable as to our arrival. Have just been looking at a squad of German prisoners on the dock, breaking stone and wheeling it away to a ship. They are under guard and look like the pictures in the papers, but all look fat and smiling. About all the women of refinement (not street peddlers, etc.) are dressed in deep mourning, so we begin to realize that we are near the theater of war.

*Wednesday, November 28th:*
We are still on board the *Madawaska*, unloading our equipment and supplies, and expect to debark some time this forenoon and march to a quarantine cantonment. West ashore yesterday for the first time at 10:00 a. m. and arranged for our transportation, rations, etc.

This is a very quaint old town (St. Nazaire), most substantially built. As you may imagine, the streets are very narrow, but kept thoroughly clean (only the main streets). There are some very good stores, particularly one department store in which I purchased a pair of gloves, which will be sent at the first opportunity, but had to guess as to size. When you write in answer to this, send me the size of gloves. Also bought some picture postcards, but the censor regulations will not permit me to send them by mail. I am dictating this while I have a little time after breakfast, waiting for the office of the transportation officer to open, as I want to get an automobile and look over our camp before we go to it. The sick were taken off the ship yesterday, including Captain Cutting, who is very much improved. Have been unable to get permission to cable and everyone on the ship is very much disappointed that we cannot cable our safe arrival.

I find that people here are more in the dark as to news of the war than are the folks at home, as it seems that what news they receive here comes from New York, Washington, London and Paris, and of course it is all censored.

Expect we may be in quarantine at least a week, and

at this writing do not know where we are to go, except that we are to go by train; the little dinky cars and engines would certainly make Robert laugh if he could see them. For example, we moved our entire command and baggage on the American train in thirty-six cars, but will have to have seventy-two cars on this French railroad. The locomotive looks like a model of the first engine ever built.

*Saturday, December 1st:*

This is Saturday night, December 1st, and I have been so busy that I have not had time to write till now, and it is almost 10:00 o'clock and the fourth night in this camp. We left the boat last Wednesday and marched about two miles to our camp and are quartered in buildings similar to the buildings at Camp American University, except that there are no floors in the buildings and the men are all sleeping on straw in their bedsocks, spread on the ground. Almost hustled my legs off that day getting rations, fuel and ovens, etc., so the men could have hot coffee and a warm supper. Our lunch we brought with us off the boat. The men were a happy lot, to get their feet on solid ground. Everything is very scarce here and we are striving to economize. I should not say everything, as food seems to be plentiful. But wood, coal, paper, milk and clothing are scarce. We had no heat for warming until today, when I managed to secure one stove for each barracks, heated by a "slack" coal and only heated evenings.

We are in quarantine and have most stringent regulations to keep all officers and men in camp, except when I give permission for them to leave on duty—or with me. We are in a camp commanded by an officer of marines—and several other organizations are here. Our sick list is improving and we hope to be out of quarantine by December 10th. Winter weather here; seems to be about like late October in Detroit, only more dampness or fog in the morning.

*Sunday Morning, December 2nd:*

This is a beautiful Sunday morning and I have come

down to the town near the dock, as we have our impedimenta in a warehouse and are moving it by motor trucks, so as to divide it up among the detachments that I am to send to their stations.

Our boat is still at the dock unloading cargo, and I took the opportunity to get one more good fresh-water shower bath. Am now writing this in the "salon" of the Hotel Bretagne—a room about ten by fourteen, containing a writing table and piano, which, with a few chairs and fireplace, completely fill it. I was up this morning while the stars were out—before Robert had looked for the "funny paper." It was so cold my toothpaste was frozen or at least so cold it would not squeeze out till I warmed it at the cook-fire.

My diary letter is so far behind that I have not recorded last Thursday yet, but will do so and I hope you may keep these letters, as I may wish to refer to them when I get back for dates and whereabouts. I am going to number the letters I have written, as I learn that No. Two may reach you before No. One does.

Last Thursday—Thanksgiving day—Major Greeley arrived at camp and surprised me, as I had talked with him from Paris on the telephone the day before. He is on the staff of the general officer at the head of the forestry department. The general officer was stationed in Detroit a year ago. You have heard me speak of him as my former instructor at West Point, General M. M. Patrick. He was so glad to learn that these two battalions had arrived that he sent Major Greeley to learn all about us, our equipment, etc. Our army is really in desperate need of lumber, fuel (wood), poles, railroad ties, bridge timber, etc. One campaign here was stopped for lack of certain wooden products. Well, he gave me my orders; so as soon as we are out of quarantine I am to send the various detachments out and will be in charge of a "district" as district commander.

We will begin work at once getting out logs, building camps, roads, cutting up the limbs for fuel—even the twigs are saved here.

Thanksgiving day was not much of a celebration here.

Worked all day, but that evening was invited to a 7:00 p. m. dinner with Major Greeley and Major Johnson, given by the "casual officers" on board our ship to us and to Captain Watson and Lieutenant McCauley of the navy. We had a good time, but it was a poor substitute for the table with you and the boys.

Thanksgiving afternoon our men and officers were addressed briefly by Chaplain Talbott of the 17th Engineers, an Episcopalian. After his talk I took the opportunity to say a few words to our men and for once in my life must have made a good one, as both the officers and men afterwards spoke of it.

We are forbidden to talk among ourselves or with civilians as to events of the war, our station, our moves, our numbers, etc., so there is very little I can write about such.

I hope and know that Nelson and Robert are good boys and a big help and comfort to you. Would like to find something to send for Christmas, but doubt if I may find anything here. At the Thanksgiving dinner was seated opposite Major Derby, who is a doctor and son-in-law of Roosevelt. Guess I will have to skip Friday and Saturday's. It was nothing but hustle anyway. Our men are feeling better and we have several ball games every afternoon—baseball and football. The sick are improving, though we lost another soldier last night of pneumonia. Captain Cutting is still in the hospital "about the same."

*Christmas Day, December, 1917:*
This day and yesterday have been for me too busy in order to enjoy them as Christmas Eve and Day should be. However, I have finally shut myself up alone to spend the rest of the afternoon with my own little family circle. I suppose we are more than 3,000 miles apart in actual distance, yet in thought I am trying to fancy that you are in the room with me and that I am to hear from Mother, Nelson and Robert how they passed Christmas Eve and whether the little souvenirs I sent arrived on time. But since you are not really here, it will be for me

to tell my story first and later on read yours—though I have not had a letter from anyone yet. It is the same with my adjutant, Captain Pill.

As I said in letter No. Ten, it would be a few days before I would have a chance to write again. Since then I have traveled more than 200 miles in a Ford—all hail the Ford! And two days besides in an antique French machine and one day additional in our own little auto ambulance—a Ford. These French roads are everywhere splendid. Otherwise I might not be so enthusiastic about the Ford. Our own transportation has not yet reached us and judging from the celerity of delivery of everything else, it will be at least a month before it does, but in the meantime we have one little Ford Red Cross ambulance received at our port of landing.

Arrived here on the eighteenth, after a most interesting, if chilly, auto drive over perfect roads, in width of pavement like our concrete roads, but with about ten feet additional of good earth road on either side. As a rule the "grand routes" are bordered on each side with trees of either sycamore, whose boughs meet in the middle of the road—or the fringe is a border of cork oak and which are generally denuded of the bark for about six or seven feet from the ground. The bark is regularly stripped for cork and in due time it grows out again.

One hundred or so years ago this country was a wide expanse of sand and sandy moraiss—a desert, but about that time experiments were made with a view of growing a forest of pine and, after years of trial and discouragement, the successful methods were found, so that the "woods" are of trees from fifty to seventy years—a species of pine resembling in appearance our "jack pine," but growing fifty to sixty feet high and with limbs about thirty feet from the ground.

The thrift of the people! All the ferns (just like our brakes) and moss and brambles are gathered annually, mixed with manure, and put back on the farms for fertilizer. The tree is cut level with the ground, the limbs down to two feet for wood and the balance gathered in baskets. Manure here passes for currency—same as in the Black Forest. Our two camps expect to have a nice fund for the purchase of knick-knacks and which will be derived from the sale of manure. Also we are going to get some piglets and grow them on our kitchen refuse, and sell them at a profit and buy more piglets, etc., etc.

The day I drove out to inspect "F" Company camp it was snowing and I am sure if you had been with me you would have pitied and yet admired the fortitude of this French womanhood. The roughest and hardest kind of work; no men to do it. Girls of fourteen, bare head and bare hands, repairing the road in the snow storm. Others at work chopping wood and driving oxen; old women, bent and worn, and boys from seven to fifteen, but no able-bodied men, only old men and men from the front invalided. Women on the railroads—section gangs. The drive for 120 miles was through these "maritime pine" forests, broken only now and then by a little old quaint and curious hamlet, but splendid roads! And we will tour them together when the war is over.

The first day after arriving here was spent in getting a general idea of "our timber" and camp, mill locations, sidings, etc. The timber had already been bought by our Forestry Service, but we must build our mills, permanent camps, stables, logging roads, side tracks and wagon roads.

The second and third days were spent in going to "F" Company—at Houeillere—and on the twenty-first my two companies "A" and "C" and headquarters arrived, but not in time to detrain them until the morning of the twenty-second. We had previously rented a motor truck and one other arrived from the 10th Engineers, with some gasoline, so that after taking the men off the trains in the morning, we had both companies at their camp sites, one four miles and one five miles, and the noon meal cooked on our army ovens. By night their tents were up, their stoves inside and fires going. The French officers could hardly believe it, for each company numbers 240 men (250 originally) and each had three baggage cars of property. They were a happy bunch of men and glad to get to work, to hear the sound of the axe and saw and fall of the tree. Both camps are, of course, right in the woods. All the French officials were, by appointment, at the station to see us march out, and before I could begin to do anything it was necessary that I call socially on all. The *prefecture*, the *commandante d'armee*, the *maire* (mayor), the *sous maire* (under-mayor), the *medicin-chef* (senior surgeon), the *chef de gare* (superintendent of railroads), the *chef gendarm* (chief of police) and finally the owner of the timber. They are all without exception most charming to meet, but beginning with yesterday they have been returning my calls. I forgot the *chef de post* (postmaster). I think you may realize that I have been these past seven days quite busy with all of these social stunts added to the regular work.

On the trip to Houeillere, we stopped over night at a village—the capital of this district (department of Landes) —Mont de Marsan. And when we take the tour after the war I hope we may be in it on a market day and view the country folk coming into town through the alley-like streets and taking up their stations on the sidewalk, where they spread out their wares for sale. It was really like that stage setting in "The Garden of Allah." I think that is the spectacular play where the cart drawn by the donkey, the camels, the burden bearers, etc., filed by. At Mont de Marsan all that was missing for a duplicate of the setting were the camels. The greatest market day of the year, the Saturday before Christmas, was the day our men arrived, so I was too busy to notice it, but all of the country folk, their chickens, ducks, geese, pigs, cows and best produce and home-made articles were from miles around located in two streets bordering the park.

This town (Dax) is a very well-known watering place and this hotel is such a grand one that I hardly feel that it is appropriate for me and my staff to stop here in war time. But it is such a contrast to the huts in which we were quartered at St. Nazaire! There we had earth floors and no doors and no heat, and then to be translated to this establishment!

Captain Pill and I are rooming together and when I

showed him his room he exclaimed, "Well, Major, the horrors of war will be when we have to leave this place." This place is something on the order of Mt. Clemens—only the waters are not sulphur. They flow in immense volume and are hot! The springs where Caesar (Julius) used to take his bath are surrounded by a rectangular, ornamental wall, with iron grated windows, through which you san see the crystal water with a perpetual cloud of steam arising. Captain Campbell claims that is what makes it so foggy here, and the fogs at Red Rock—Rockland—are not a circumstance. At this spring the townsfolk come for blocks with their pitchers to get hot water. Within a stone's throw are the old Roman ramparts, still standing in splendid preservation, about twenty feet high.

I have my headquarters in the town and one company on one side about four miles away and the other on another side about five miles distant. The headquarters detachment, about forty men, are encamped—where do you think?—well, I got permission to pitch our tents in the "Arena"—a Spanish bull ring, surrounded with raised seats all constructed of concrete, similar to our ball park, except the diameter of the ring is only about 150 feet, but is the best camping place we will ever get. Under the concrete raised benches are rooms where we store our baggage, also toilet rooms; and where they kept the bulls and horses we are going to keep our horses, pigs, auto trucks, automobile, and the best of all—one of the hot springs is but a few feet from the entrance. A circular, concrete wall with only two entrances encloses the place—a most admirable place for a little camp. When we shut the big door we are hidden from the curious, though friendly, public, which has been flocking to look at us so much that I had the mayor put up a notice that it was forbidden to enter the arena without permission from him. Soon we shall have the arena connected with electric light and our own telephone to the two camps—and then we will be settled.

My men have just "picked up" a man in the uniform of a Canadian and he is either demented or a spy, so I sent him to the town "bastile" and will soon have to go and investigate him.

Just advised that tomorrow we get twenty sacks of mail. I have not had a letter from you yet. If those twenty sacks fail to have several I will be disappointed. I heard also that our boat, the *Madawaska*, had not sailed on the twentieth, so the long first letter I wrote will not reach you for some days yet.

This has not been like Christmas for us. I tried to make it a little like it last night. I gave a dinner to my staff and the two company commanders—ten of us. We had roast turkey and plum pudding and the plum pudding was real home-like, but there was not much jollity at the table and I knew that everyone's heart was back somewhere in the States. I called the roll by states and it was:

Vermont, one, Lieutenant Doctor Aldrich.
Maine, one, Lieutenant Freedman.
New York, one, Lieutenant Dentist.
California, one captain.
Pennsylvania, one captain.
New Jersey, one captain.
Wisconsin, one captain.
Michigan, one major, myself.

We had the Stars and Stripes and Tri-color hanging and toasted both flags, "our wives, sisters and sweethearts," the President of France and President Wilson. Tell Nelson that the plum pudding lacked the hard sauce.

Have been to see about that Canadian and will telegraph the commanding officer of the Canadian forces in this district to send for him. The fellow is O. K., but without funds and is off in his upper story.

Have received another letter of commendation, which I enclose, so you see that we are behaving ourselves. Have not seen a paper in over a week. There is no news in them when we do see them here. Just extracts from American papers. All of the French people seem downhearted at the collapse of Russia.

Tomorrow I have to make about a ten-mile tramp through the timber and around the lines of the block that

Captain Elam is to cut and have left a call for 5:00 o'clock, so my girl and kiddies, good night.

*Sunday, December 30, 1917:*
This is in answer to your Thanksgiving letter and is being written as indicated by the Y. M. C. A. symbol above. Have driven in a French automobile 128 miles in the last twenty-four hours and am in one of the largest cities in France.* The hotel is so cold—for lack of coal—that I have looked up this place so as to spend this Sunday afternoon with you and the boys (and Jim and Nellie) at a place where I would not have to wear my overcoat to keep warm.

I wish my descriptive faculties would permit me to picture this Y. M. C. A. to you, so that you could really see it. It is the third story of a very large building overlooking one of the "Places"—or plazas or squares. After climbing the three stairways, all of stone steps common to all of the buildings, I entered a room in which was an American girl at a table—the information desk—and in the room were several U. S. sailors and soldiers. On the walls were placards, being invitations to the different churches and to an entertainment to be given New Year's. Looking through two adjoining rooms, I saw in one a large, long table, at which soldiers and sailors were writing letters, and in the other room, with clouds of cigarette smoke our "boys" were seated at tables, eating real ice cream and cakes, visiting and listening to the piano alternately rendering a hymn or "Dixie" or other airs. Just now the air is "Long, Long Ago," and do you wonder that it has caused me to pause, close my eyes, and see that old school room in Grayling where we used to sing it when you played the organ. . . . I am writing this in the little private office of the secretary, a triangular room about eight by ten—but with a fire-place with a *real coal fire!*

Your letter of November 29th reached me December 26th. Tell the boys that I enjoyed both of their letters and hope to receive more soon. That cartoon was a pat reminder of the evenings with Nelson and the algebra at

---
*Paris—which Major Hartwick visited during his trip to General Pershing's headquarters at Chaumont.

Fontanet Courts, Washington, D. C.—am keeping it as a souvenir. Tell the boys that if I get the kodak I will certainly take some pictures for them, but it is against the rules to mail them and I will have to take them home with me.

In the only paper that I have seen in a week—the Paris edition of the New York Herald—I was pleased to read of the conviction of Kaltschmidt. I wonder if Uncle Sam will not have to enlarge the federal prisons.

You are probably wondering where I am writing this letter and I hope you may guess, although I am not permitted to advise you. I am about 100 miles away from my headquarters, here on official business. Think you know from other letters where that town is, and I think I wrote you about the surroundings of our headquarters camp and the hotel in which I had been staying.

Near the hotel is a large "Casino" in which during peace time there was a music hall, gaming tables, cafe and theater. On Christmas Eve we were all invited to the movies and though the explanations were in French I was able to understand it and enjoy it. But it was pitiful when after the performance the soldiers tried to sing the Star Spangled Banner to the accompaniment of French violinist—a young lady who is stopping at the hotel and who was good enough to play for our Christmas dinner—but the rendering of that National Hymn of ours was certainly painful. . . .

While writing the above one of the secretaries entered the room, followed by an American "Jackie," and closed the door. I could not help listening to the conversation, a most pitiful story about a nineteen-year-old Belgian girl, whose father and brother were killed by the Huns, and this poor girl left alone. Well, this "Jackie," who is an American citizen now, is married and has a home in Newton, Massachusetts, was educated at the Belgian Military School and is a Master Mason. He showed me letters from his lodge and from Senator Weeks. He had gone to school with the girl in Brussels when a boy. He saw her on the street here, recognized her, and received the story from her lips of her work and despair. So he came to the Y. M. C. A. for help. Poor girl—well, I shelled out ten francs and am going to try to help her more. I have never seen her, but if she were in Detroit as an assistant to Miss Stevens she could earn a living and do some good. Her case is one of thousands. The Kaiser should suffer!

Day before yesterday there came to my camp a Canadian soldier who acted very queerly and I thought he might be a spy, so turned him over to the French military. They kept him a day and found that he was "dippy" from shell-shock, so turned him over to the Canadian headquarters at the base. One of the statements he made to me was that he was "traveling out of Paris for the firm." Evidently he had been a Canadian traveling man before the war.

We had two inches of snow yesterday and it was beautiful while touring that 100 or so miles over perfect roads, bordered on each side with tall sycamore or cork oaks, their boughs laden with snow and the roadway perfectly white for miles ahead. I am enclosing a pencil list of the contents of the comfort bag from Mrs. Woodrow Wilson.

Have had an invitation from the gentleman who sold us the timber to go trout fishing in the spring. He speaks about as good English as I speak French, and he said, "It ees jolie to catc zee troot wiz zee flee." Do you get it? To catch the trout on a fly is fun. Expect to return to my base on New Year's Day.

*January 12, 1918:*

When this trip shall have been finished I shall have traveled, since January 1st, 1,412 miles and will be glad to rest awhile. Have finished my work in this town and have about three-quarters of an hour to spare before starting for the train, so instead of trying to see the sights I would rather visit with you.

There is no snow here, but when I was at General Pershing's headquarters there was plenty of it and I enjoyed watching our soldiers coasting down an extremely long hill on what looked like real American bob-sleds.

And at another place where the French are making quantities of munitions on a Thursday the square was crowded with children and the boys reminded me of the boys on Edison Avenue, Detroit, because snowballs were flying through the air. I learned that they do not go to school on Thursdays and Sundays, but go on Saturdays.

The first mill* to get started by the twentieth was by "B" Company. They have been running since January 5th, and shipped their first car of lumber to the front the day I was with them. They are located near our central supply station and so were able to get the machinery. Cars are so scarce here that if the rest of the companies wait for American mills it will be about March 1st before we are sawing. However, I am trying to buy or rent some French mills and if I do we will be grinding out boards within a couple of weeks at the other two companies. I have a half company of the 2nd Battalion under me now— about sixty miles from my headquarters.

I am collecting some of the French "posters" for their loans—like our Liberty Loan. They are very scarce now and are being collected by the book shops and sold. Wish you might collect some of our American posters. I am going to write to Wilson Staley or Mr. De Graff to get some and send them to you.

Visited Notre Dame Cathedral, but it is not as when we were here—not over a score of candles burning in the whole edifice. It was so dark and gloomy I hurried out. There was nothing to see. The Louvre was also closed, but I went through that store called the Louvre and it was crowded. The town is so dark at night that you might fancy yourself in some country village were it not for the people passing on the sidewalk. Went with Colonel Pickart (from Detroit), a national guard officer, and with Colonel Hickok, who was a second lieutenant with me in the 9th Cavalry at Fort Robinson in 1893, to the Casino to see Gaby Deslys. Price $2.50 and the show not worth it. Quite on the order of our "comic opera," but more akin to a "variety show." Once is enough. She is the creature for whom the King of Portugal showed himself the fool.

*Of French manufacture.

Yesterday the French on the train were all enthusiastic over Mr. Wilson's address to our Congress, wherein he enumerated the fourteen conditions for peace. Of course, the condition calling for the return of Alsace and Lorraine pleases them—and also the reference to Belgium. Quite often I am asked by them: "How long do you think the war will last?" and "How many soldiers will America have over here this spring?" and they are disappointed when I shrug my shoulders and answer, "*Je ne sais pas.*" It is a gigantic job and we are preparing for it on a huge scale. At a supply camp that is now being built where I was yesterday the main side track is eight miles long, and we are building a huge ice plant there, etc. My hands are so cold I can hardly write—no heat in this room—I must get ready for the train.

*Somewhere in France, January 15, 1918:*
Have for the first time since we left Washington had my desk actually cleared. It is now 7:30 in the evening (about 1:00 o'clock in the afternoon in Detroit) and I am alone in my tent with a good wood fire snapping in the Sibley stove for company. When one side (of me) gets too warm the other side is cold, yet this tent is quite cozy so long as the fire is going. Our camp is very still just now, because most of the detachment have gone on pass to town. Have only about thirty-six men and seven officers here—one company five miles away and another four miles, another sixty and another about 450 miles away. Have just received the latest paper, yesterday's one-sheet newspaper from Paris, the European edition of the Chicago Tribune, but before I read it will have a visit with you. Guess I wrote about the New Year's dinner I had at Bordeaux with General Scott—Mr. Vincent Astor at the table and the Y. M. C. A. there.

I am sending under separate cover some illustrated papers, one a paper of the Royal Flying Corps of England, that will please Robert, and one a compilation of placards that the Germans posted in Belgium and France. The last page of the latter is worth reading to get an idea of the spirit of the French people in the "Lost Provinces."

Today has been a beautiful day here and a great change from the weather of last week. The first real sunshine that I have seen in what I have heard called "sunny France." It has been rainy, snowy, cloudy, foggy, misty and muddy and repeat—till today. It was so clear we could see the snow-clad peaks of the mountains about forty miles to the southwest.

Tomorrow I take the French military *commandante*, the mayor, the under-mayor and others to inspect the camps of Company "A" and Company "B" and they are counting on having a great meal there. Well, we will not disappoint them, for the captains have been advised that we are coming.

Heard today that Colonel Mitchell and the other two battalions of the Twentieth are on their way over here, so if it be true I shall take it up with him as planned about transferring to the Ordnance.* Wish it were so I could walk home, for there is more danger on the ocean going to America than coming over here, because the homeward bound vessels are not so well protected. We have one mill running—Company "B," 1st Battalion— but am afraid the other companies will not get their machinery for some weeks. It certainly looked good to see the saw slicing off the boards. The engine, boiler and carriage were sent from America for us, but the saw and other parts were purchased here.

Am sending you with this a placard, being one of many seen on the walls all over France, to combat the curse of alcohol. I took this off a wall in a station by permission. It says that alcohol—"cognac, eau-de-vie," etc., are as much of an enemy to France as the Boche, whose head is at the top.

*Somewhere in France, January 17, 1918:*

Have written the last two letters to the boys, so this evening's visit is with you. About a half dozen of the soldiers of my headquarters detachment have been singing a sort of moonlight serenade and it has been quite a treat. One of them has been a professional singer.

*Major Hartwick, while at Camp American University, had received a promise from Colonel Mitchell that he should be transferred to the ordnance department as soon as the opportunity came.

Sitting in their tent, the door open, the light shining through, and the other tents alongside it, has made quite a theatrical scene, and I wish you were here to enjoy it. We are encamped in the arena and the moon shining down over the circular, walled banks of seats in our tents is quite a picture. Have had our first good weather these last three days and today it has been like summer—no overcoat—the women sitting out of doors, knitting in the sun, with no wraps and no head covering.

Have accomplished about all I can do here until our machinery comes. Am going to try tomorrow to rent or buy two small French mills. Have tried to learn if Colonel Mitchell has left the U. S. yet or not, but can learn nothing except "to hold his mail." If you could get over here with the boys this is a splendid winter resort. I am sending you some postcards showing you what the place is like. It would be a good place for a short sojourn for grandpa, but on account of the submarines it is not to be thought of. I really do not fancy going back on that account, for the navy does not seem to guard so thoroughly the ships returning as coming. However, when Colonel Mitchell comes will try and hold him to his promise. The natives here do not think the war will last this year out—"the wish is father to the thought."

The enclosed "ritual" I am sending is for a sort of vigilance society* that our soldiers have formed among themselves. We officers are not supposed to know about it. It has come about because I published the order to them that the extent of liberty, privileges, etc., that they would get would depend on their behavior, so they are looking to it.

Yesterday the military *commandante* of the French accompanied me on an inspection of the two camps and was very much pleased with all he saw. Today a Canadian colonel with his two captains called. They are making an inspection and during his visit I learned that

---

* "The Most Loyal and Secret Flock of Ducks," whose ritual provided an application of scrub-brush and soap, to be followed by immersion, to the "duck" who "flew too high and wild." The motto was, "Be a good duck and sin no more" and the official call was "Quack! Quack!"

he is a brother of Doctor Battie, the oculist in Detroit, and that he belongs to the Exchange Club.

*Saturday the 19th:*
Was interrupted Thursday and have not had a chance to finish this till this—Saturday—evening. Am sending by separate mail through the French store some postcards that show the life and points of interest around here.

The Casino building you will see is a very beautiful structure. Before the war it held grand opera, a cafe, billiard hall and various gaming rooms. Now nothing but an occasional moving picture. The manager has offered us two rooms for use of the officers for a club when we are in town and we have been pleased to accept. We shall have a reading room, also a billiard and music room, combined with billiard table and piano furnished. Then when we receive the graphophone you have sent, we will install it also. Rooms will be open from 2:00 to 9:30 p. m.

Have heard a rumor that the 3rd and 4th Battalions will arrive at some port January 25th. Hope it is true.

*January 25, 1918:*
This has been another day of perfect sunshine. It seems now that we are being repaid this last ten days in sunshine for all of the disagreeable weather we had previous to that time and since landing here. Was out riding this afternoon, the first time, for pleasure only— unless for the exercising of the horse. Have three of them for my headquarters, but none of them would draw any kind of a prize at a show for riding horses. However, it was a most pleasant jaunt and I wished many times that you were with me on the "pinkish grey" pony (or one like it) that we had at Huachuca.

The ride I chose led through the narrow, alley-like streets of this quaint old town, past the multi-colored, though soft toned, stucco-walled "villas," to the levee that borders and follows the river "Adour." The riding path is about ten feet wide on top of the levee embankment, which is fringed on both sides with the sycamore, cork oak and other native trees. It was like a day in

June at home. The meadows along the river were a beautiful green carpet animated by sheep, cattle and geese. Invalided soldiers were out in numbers, strolling with a *camarade*—usually a sister or sweetheart. At one place I passed at the foot of the embankment an old man, a shepherd, lying at the foot of a large tree, its roots for a pillow, taking a nap in the warm sun with two dogs by his side. And how startled and amazed he looked as he gazed up at me when a growl from his dog awakened him and he felt the shock of my horse's hoofs on the ground above him! The pussy-willows were out, hanging by my side in many places, and I thought of Robert, and how long it will be before he will be bringing in some from the woods the other side of Hamilton Boulevard.

We have been filled with a little pride for our country folk back home to read in the Paris paper that by the President's order the factories were shut down for five days and that, though more than a million workmen were laid off, that there was no disorder. Guess America is getting into this game in the proper spirit. But I hope it will not be felt as it is here. For example, I visited ten mill yards (saw mills) and found women rolling the logs on the carriage, at the saws, piling lumber in the yard and loading it on cars. They are even in the railroad yards, unloading heavy rails from the cars, and some of them are girls not much past sixteen or seventeen.

Received a Christmas box January 21st from Detroit Commandery No. 1 and its contents helped me entertain that day at our headquarters luncheon a French visiting "liaison" officer. He is one of the corps that assists in ironing our wrinkles that get in the relationships between our armies and he was seemingly disappointed that we had no troubles to be straightened out. Oh, that box contained:

1 pair stockings, with a pipe (briar) inside of one stocking.
20 packages of cigarettes.
12 packages of tobacco.
12 packages of cigarette papers.

1 pair knit gloves.
1 large package of raisins (Spanish).
1 package of dates (California).
1 dozen sticks of licorice.
1 can of prepared coffee (Geo. Washington brand).
1 can plum pudding.
1 can Oxo soup tablets.
20 nickel packages of Butternut chewing gum.
1 package of 24 cakes of Hershey's chocolate.

Had to teach the French officers how to use the chewing gum.

Am enclosing copy of order that General McClure sent me and that he issues to all of the incoming organizations. You will note in paragraph thirteen why he sent me a copy.* It will give us some good advertising among the troops that land at that base. Also copy of a report that shows that up to the tenth of this month, my battalion was leading all of the other troops in this base. You will notice that our record is clean.

Our Y. M. C. A. secretary has come and I have had to take him out to the two camps where his station is to be. At one we have built a hut about thirty feet by ninety, and as soon as we get the floor in it will be ready for the entertainment of the men. We are borrowing the lumber from a French mill.

Last Sunday, with the two company commanders, was invited to "breakfast" at 12:30. I enclose the invitation from the gentleman who sold the timber that we are lumbering.

We expect it will produce about 15,000 M feet of lumber and he got practically $500,000 for it—over $30 per M on the stump—an inheritance—and he has the money already. Well, the "breakfast" lasted till 2:00 p. m., so for war time it was some breakfast. He apologized and said the priest had cautioned the attendants at church that morning that they should not eat much from now on—but it was in our honor.

---

*Paragraph 13 was reference to letter of commendation given by General McClure to Major Hartwick in appreciation of the behavior of the latter's command at St Nazaire. This order is reproduced on another page.

saying that our work is too important. On return from "C" Company President Shanklin must have a light lunch before going to bed, so we chatted till midnight. He is a remarkable man and ranks very high among our university presidents. He was on the faculty for years with President Wilson at Wesleyan; and told me of his visit with Mr. Wilson shortly before he sailed, and also of his visit and dinner with General Wood the other night at Paris, and some confidential "inside information." He said that General Wood's wound is healing beautifully and that it was a miraculous escape from death. He seemed to warm up to me merely because I went to the train to meet him and looked after him while he was here. At his last stop previous to this, the secretaries of the "Y" where he spoke did not meet him and, *worse*, permitted the canteen window to be open and sales in progress while he was speaking. So the old gentleman was somewhat discouraged when he arrived here. Of course I did not know of his experience, but had all of my officers and men assembled to listen to him—*by order*—merely because it was a mark of respect that a man on his mission deserved. So that evening he said, after his cup of chocolate, "Major, you seem a sort of kindred spirit. Please tell me frankly, do you think my work is worth while? I am needed back at the college, because so many others are in the war service too and also away from college." And I was pleased to answer him, "Yes, most assuredly," and begged of him to make a report of the ungentlemanly and senseless conduct of those secretaries. His daughter is over here in Y. M. C. A. work and his son in the American service. You know his college is ranked, or its faculty is ranked, among the first five for prominence and influence. It was my job to introduce him to the audience at each meeting—two nights. Then today I was asked to be the speaker at the Sunday services at each company —one this morning and one this evening. So it was up to me and I was really thankful when after the services this morning and the company officers came up to me separately, told me I had made a good talk and thanked me. But I am sure if there was any merit, it was on account of the subject. Some of my remarks, those I can remember, were:

"When Mr. Brook asked me to speak to you today, my natural impulse was to beg off, to tell him the truth—that I am no speaker. But I realized that, in this game over here, we must all do whatever we may to help out, so I will be at least—as newspaper men say—a space-filler. He told me the subject should be about the annual banquets that the Y. M. C. A. have been having these last few years back in America—and that took me back to my own home town, Detroit, Michigan, and into our "Y" there. And, by the way, there are many things that we are proud of as citizens of Detroit, and the Detroit Y. M. C. A. building is one of the largest and best equipped in the world. If you are, when we get back home, a visitor to Detroit, visit our "Y" and if you stay over night get a room there. Well, for some three years now boys of twelve years or over may attend our 'fathers' day' annual banquets; and at least once a year the 'old man' can hear some kindly things said of him. It has been my good fortune to have had one boy sit at that table now for three years—and this year there will be two, the youngest just twelve years.

"You baseball fans know of Sam Crawford, the star right fielder of the Tigers? Well, Sam is always the stellar attraction at our banquets, and perhaps that is why the boys are always so anxious to be at the table. Not that Sam is a good speaker, he is not—almost as poor as am I—but he is some ball player. His home is in Detroit and we know him. He always plays the game fair, and we know him, not only as a ball player, but as a man—morally one of the cleanest. He always gives the boys a two-minute talk on clean living and on playing the game of life on the square, and it is quite natural that the boys listen more attentively to him than to their own dads. By the way, some baseball news. We of Detroit will regret to learn that Sam, after playing on our team for, I am sure, over fifteen years, has been given his release, but we hope he will continue to be one of Detroit's honored citizens.

"Now, a word as to this honored function of 'fathers' day.' We, over here, may not have a banquet, but we can let dad know that he is not forgotten. Do you know what it means to a fellow to get a letter from his boys? Well, thank God, I do! Just a few days ago I got one from that twelve-year-old boy of mine and it is a pleasure to me to read it over and re-read it once again. He told me, in his boyish way, of their Christmas dinner at home, with the grandfather and all the uncles, aunts and cousins. It must have been a long course dinner, for the family was so large that they had it at the club, and my boy had to sit awhile after the plum pudding while the men smoked, for he wrote 'it was the longest dinner I ever had or that I ever hope to have.'

"Why am I ringing in such personal matters? Simply to say that you, who are so lucky as to still have a father on earth, should, as I know you will, write him a letter, if not tonight, very soon. I saw a letter written by an American 'dad' to one of the boys over here. Perhaps some of you may have read it also, but even so, it is so good that I want to read it to all of you. It was published in the paper of the 18th Engineers—'The Spiker.' . . . . " and then I read to them the letter enclosed and attached hereto. I think this letter "saved my life" and of course was the only good part of what I had to say to them.

But you see the variety of work that goes with my job. The busier I am, the better for me, for then I will not get homesick. Yet I do like to get a little more time to write, also I would like to do as the other officers are doing, take regular French lessons.

Just received the "Detroiter," also two more "Digests" —the last one dated February 2nd came on the 16th, best mail service yet, also another bunch of Washington Posts. Captain Pill got a nice box, salted peanuts, dates candied and candy. Candy here is scarce and what I get from the Y. M. C. A., creamed chocolate drops, cost two cents apiece.

Your letter of the sixteenth of January was received the twelfth of February and so this is the answer to it.

It told that you were still having the exceedingly cold weather and the difficulties of the coal situation, also told of Nelson's experience with Jack Frost and I hope long before this that he has gotten over the effects. And so you are short of sugar too now back in America? From the papers it seems that you back home are doing all you can to deprive yourselves of everything that will help to help the army and allies over here.

Am glad the boys are taking dancing lessons and hope that they will be able to teach me the new steps when I get home. I saw on the last cover that we received of the Saturday Evening Post a picture of a dancing party and was reminded of Nelson's remark that there was one boy who was a bigger boob than he.

You wrote about the newspapers censuring the secretary of war and said part of the blame is on account of Congress. Yes, I agree with you, but also our people all over. In this connection I remember a conversation that I had with Mr. J—. It was at that banquet about two years ago. He pooh-poohed the idea of a larger army than we then had, or any more military preparations, and rather sneered at me for not agreeing with him. Yet he thinks, or seems to think, his judgment is ahead of others. I remember he took an active part in the round-table discussions at the club a year ago. Well, he is the type of citizen who is to blame for Uncle Sam's not being prepared *a year ago.* Of course, Secretary Baker himself was a pacifist before he got into the war. Practical pacifism is all right, but not the know-nothing kind. Some day I want to remind Mr. J— of his wisdom. Before our citizens a year ago should have talked against a larger army, they should have read more "on the other side" of the subject.

*In France, February 21, 1918:*
In the last chapter I did not tell you that General Scott, who is in command of this base with headquarters at B— (Bordeaux) dropped in on us by automobile with his staff —or part of it—on his way to P—, (Paris) where there is an aviation school. The next day, on his return, he took

lunch with us and of course we had an extra good feed. Was glad of the opportunity to pilot him out to the camp of "A" Company in his car—a Winton limousine—and it was the fastest I have ever gone in an auto—sixty-eight miles per. I didn't think it strange that the day before he had brought us, when he arrived, on the running board, a sheep that his car had killed a half-hour before. Well, he was very well pleased with his inspection of the camp and I was glad when he complimented Captain Elam. It is laid out as per my order, but the captain keeps it spick and span.

Yesterday was passed on a trip by the Ford inspecting a French saw mill near Bordeaux for a major of the 10th Engineers. It was very cold when we started at 6:30 in the morning. I wore your sweater, then my blouse, then my raincoat and next my overcoat, the wristlets you knit, fur-lined gloves and a winter cap, also two blankets over my lap and feet. You see the nights are cold—two inches of ice on the water bucket outside my tent, but as soon as the sun peeps through the clouds, it gets real warm and, when not driving, too warm for an overcoat. We passed many flowers in bloom in the yards of pretty "villas." One arbor of ——? (think it is spelled camellia), red and pink that made me think of that rose arbor we saw at Winnetka last summer. Pine trees, cedar trees, fir trees and palm trees—also oak and sycamore—hills and valleys and splendid roads. Found the mill, but disapproved of its purchase. However, was pleased that the trip took me so near to B———, which is only about three miles from B———. The last B——— is on the ocean, and the most beautiful ocean resort I have ever seen. The late King Ed had a palace there—Ed the VII. I wish we could spend some days there together. The finest rooms, with bath, and meals included, room overlooking ocean, for thirty francs, $6, per day. Certainly is cheap enough. There are many people there, even now, English and Spanish and French soldiers, officers on leave. But it is very quiet there now. A magnificent beach for surf bathing and I don't believe there is any fear of sharks. Just now it is too cold for bathing. From July 1st to October 1st is the season. I bought the best mantilla in the largest store there, but I am not satisfied with it and have arranged for a certain person who is going down into Spain to get me another. I think he will have to smuggle it, so I was told, but I do not know it and I do not know him. Hope it will arrive in time for your birthday.

Am sending you some colored photos of the resort; they are real pretty. Photographed in colors, so they say, which I doubt, but anyway the coloring is not overdone, but really true to nature. Also sending a book of *poste-cartes*.

Am also enclosing in this some invitations such as we are sending out to a list of officials and citizens here. It was necessary to ask the French military *commandante* here to submit us a list of those whom we should properly invite as especial guests. You see, we are to have a "field day" for the soldiers—company and individual contests. The day before a baseball game between a team from the 1st Battalion of the 10th Engineers and our 1st Battalion team. Also the band of the 4th Battalion will be in attendance. I am sending a large truck, improvised into a "rubber-neck," for the band—not for them, but for the freight they brought over for us (among it the graphophones). You see, we are going to give George a two-day celebration—on the twenty-third and twenty-fourth. Have extended a general invitation to the populace and special invitations (for refreshments—army coffee, real white bread and sandwiches). Expect about 200 French notables and their families. So I know I will not have a chance to write a letter next Sunday. We expect twelve officers from the other camps whom we shall also entertain. It has been something for the men to look forward to for about a month and a good thing, too, to keep them contented. They have been practicing for the contests and selecting their representatives for some time. Am enclosing invitations to the lumber family.

## "Last Letters"

The last messages from Major Hartwick were those dictated on the twenty-fifth of March to his wife and two boys. These were dictated while he was confined to his bed and were very brief. The letters in part, follow:

"MY DEAR GIRL:

"Since I wrote you only the day before yesterday there is nothing hardly I can think of to say, especially since I am enclosing in this two letters for the boys.

"It must be that the cold weather has eventually deserted Michigan and that life can be more in keeping with the motto of Detroit, where 'Life is worth living.'

"The letter from Robert is a literary gem, if hardly an orthographical one. We are not getting now all of the good things over here in the markets that I wrote you about soon after we landed. They have no sugar, but the liquid saccharine; they have no white flour and if there is any quantity of one thing that there is to be had in plenty it is meat.

"I certainly appreciate your compliment that some of my letters do have some literary merit, but I think you must be mistaken, for you will remember how many times you have told me that my letters at home were altogether too matter-of-fact, and I think it must be the news in the letters and not any especial literary value, for one does not have any time over here to sit down and think out any letter, but has to shove it off as fast as his thoughts may flow. Hope you will not take any offense at this last remark, or not feel any neglect thereat, because you will have to confess that even if my letters are written hurriedly, they are long enough to make up for the other."

"DEAR NELSON:

"I wrote you just the other day, although I do not believe it was in answer to any letter from you, as your letter of January 19th just received is, I think, the most recent one I have received from you.

"I wish to compliment you upon your improvement in letter-writing and also on your penmanship, and I hope that both you and Robert passed in your recent examinations.

"I have received the records that you sent for the Victrola, but guess I have already told you that. They are very good records and have been much enjoyed, but I am keeping the one record for my own.

"Tell Robert that if he did not get a Christmas calendar it was some mistake. If I did not have his name on it it was simply not intentional.

"I have already told you at the beginning of this letter when your letter was received, so you see it took for this letter a little over two months, but other letters have come on quicker time.

"I also have written you previously that I have my old army pants over here with me, so that if you need some for the Cadet Corps, you will have to buy a pair."

"Dear Bobbie:
"Your letter of January 20th was a long time in reaching me, as I did not get it until March 24th. However, if it was so long in coming I have enjoyed it just that much more and you may tell Mother that I shall certainly save it. Also tell Mother that this letter is being dictated and typewritten because I have been directed by the Medical Officer to go to bed for a couple of days at least. He has pronounced it grippe, so I should be thankful that it is nothing worse, and also thankful that I have someone who can take down the letter, as otherwise when I do get up I shall be so busy that some days would pass before I could write you.

"Your description of the severe winter and the deep snow is the best I have received, as you could really make me feel how cold it was and see the deep piles of snow. Am glad that you liked the little presents that I was able to send and that you got your pick.

"I know you did not get discouraged on account of your first experience at dancing school—just remember when little discouragements come that when you tackle the job the next time you are going to do it better, and then you will do so. I hope you will know all of the new dancing steps, so when I get home you and Mother can teach them to me.

"I guess I anticipated your desire for some French stamps, so I sent a very good collection a long time ago. It will not be easy, however, to get any Spanish stamps.

"This isn't much of a letter and not as long as your nice letter deserves, but when you remember that I am thinking of it in bed and have still got a headache you will overlook its shortness."

www.ingramcontent.com/pod-product-compliance
Lightning Source LLC
Chambersburg PA
CBHW070455090426
42735CB00012B/2561